The Bronx Bombers

Word Search

Puzzle Book

The Bronx Bombers
Word Search
Puzzle Book

Puzzles by Michael Norton

Reedy Press, PO Box 5131, St. Louis, MO 63139, USA

No part of this publication may be reproduced or transmitted in
any form or by any means, electronic or mechanical, including
photocopy, recording, or any information storage and retrieval
system, without permission in writing from the publisher.

Permissions may be sought directly from Reedy Press at the above
mailing address or via our website at www.reedypress.com.

Library of Congress Control Number: on file

ISBN: 978-1-933370-34-7

puzzles by Michael Norton
cover by Kevin Belford

For information on all Reedy Press publications visit our website at
www.reedypress.com.

Printed in the United States of America
08 09 10 11 12   5 4 3 2 1

It Was a Very Good Year

```
M I N A M K C I W B O B A I Z
C A R O L U G A K O L A M C E
H U S T T S H Y P E O J I N R
A T R E S T P R A T E W E Z E
R I T T M E U I S T E S U I P
L M K O Y A V H K I L H M C O
I B I O B O J L K E G O B Y D
E U N T O B U N I R O R O E I
H R O W J C A N O S A W C B L
A K T I O T Y M G I E M E T E
Y E A C S R V D I U D V R N M
E R P Y R I S O N J E F A D Y
S U D E K U D Y F A N H I D O
C N J Y D A R B F F I L C T S
A R U S S S P R I N G E R T E
```

TIM BURKE	JERRY NIELSEN
RUSS SPRINGER	BOB WICKMAN
CURT YOUNG	CHARLIE HAYES
DAVE SILVESTRI	DION JAMES
ANDY STANKIEWICZ	MARK HUTTON
JIM ABBOTT	ANDY COOK
SPIKE OWEN	MELIDO PEREZ

Fielders of Dreams

```
Y L D O K E V I N M M A H A T
E E Y Y L G N I T T A M N O D
K N F I Z O S E K A H R N Q E
C N R F E R P E T E E Y U S L
I S C I I S I Y E L F E R E T
N A H W Q R W C S E T E C L T
E K T S W U G A R A Y I I U I
O A A A T A E N D M C L O T L
R T M R T E A W E E D N V N N
Y A S B K N V K I K B E H N A
R E I I D A I E R L N O S A Y
A B M E V M B U K A S T G R R
G O Z E R E P T R E B O R G B
O R I A C L E U G I M I N T S
F R E A D M Y P P E R P M A Y
```

WADE BOGGS

KEN GRIFFEY

ENRIQUE WILSON

BRYAN LITTLE

LENN SAKATA

GARY ROENICKE

TONY FERNANDEZ

DON MATTINGLY

STEVE KEMP

ROBERT PEREZ

MIKE EASLER

MIKE MYERS

KEVIN MMAHAT

MIGUEL CAIRO

We Love 'Em

```
S C O T T L U S A D E R S R C
M C S A A M N I V E K U O T U
E A O K E I T H E N R N N M R
I L R T H E O D U O K E A R T
S V L D T U E L L O G M O B
N T A I I S P Y I N M R R W L
I R E N O C A M V I M E G A E
K Y O V I T K N A P Y G I B F
D T J R E O T W D L R P K S A
A K E D W F I M O E J O L D R
E E A S E S A V A O R T A A Y
V W K D T A U R O D D S H Y P
E I O G A L Y E R E D S O W L
T C O A L R O N O H T O O N I
S D N O S A M M I J F A X N C
```

RON KLIMKOWSKI

KEVIN MAAS

WADE TAYLOR

SCOTT SANDERSON

DICK WOODSON

CURT BLEFARY

ERIC PLUNK

SCOTT LUSADER

TOREY LOVULLO

STEVE FARR

ELLIOTT MADDOX

JIM MASON

STEVE ADKINS

Yankee Style

```
T H G I R W E S A H C O L I E
B G C K C A M O W Y E L O O D
E I N C O J O S S I U L O H O
E A D O H A R L I E T R O O I
R N U D L R O N O H A M D M Z
L K I E W E I G R Z E M N E Z
E E C T A C C S I R A Y O R I
I N W I L S O N B E T E M I T
U N E E O H N U E R E V R D N
G E K O N A S E L R I E O R A
N D I J C H S T A N R T L I C
O Y M Y R V A S Y L S E T G Y
R O D S I R G K N A R F T O D
A N O S R E F F E J N A T S N
A E K R A L C E C A R O H U A
```

DOOLEY WOMACK   HORACE CLARKE

STAN JEFFERSON   WILSON BETEMIT

CHASE WRIGHT   CHRIS BRITTON

ANDY CANNIZARO   IAN KENNEDY

TERRENCE LONG   AARON GUIEL

HOMER BUSH   LUIS SOJO

Dude Through the Decades

```
N C N O T L I M A H E V E T S
F R A N K C R O S E T T I K S
W B H R A N S Y A M L R A C A
A I T D L R I L F F O M P H L
R L D H A H E C H T I N A I A
E L D I G R U C K E S L T T H
F S O E L I R B N G R I D R E
E T T C S I R I B E R V O E G
I A S I O Y E B N E P E N K R
K F N V N C T I Y C L S E A O
E F E Y K R F O O R H L Y N E
V O D I I F A V I N R A O O G
E R O N N O C O Y D D A P O R
T D I T A H D I Z L A E H I W
S H K E V I N T H O M P S O N
```

BILL STAFFORD

STEVE HAMILTON

PADDY O'CONNOR

GEORGE HALAS

FRANK CROSETTI

KEVIN THOMPSON

S. (SCOTT) KAMIENIECKI

HAL RENIFF

HARRY BRIGHT

CARL MAYS

STEVE KIEFER

NICK GREEN

DARRIN CHAPIN

Names From the 90s

```
N A Y D S E N O J Y M M I J E
T A B A A J Y R R U P Y E I C
D T Z O N L O D W A T F B I R
A N I O N D E H E L F V K E I
S D S W N D Y P N R H A D N C
W Y I R E I A H O H I N O A S
E O G E E K P B A L A S L M N
N L A D K W I S A W L B V E S
D L V R N N O M E E K E Y G T
I E I A S R L L N O B I Y A A
S M N O H F A F B M R R N L N
M E N U W W F C O E I A E S R
M A C O M E C H N S K N V C F
O R L I J R S T C O L I E L O
T G J A H M O R B E T O M G A
```

JOHN HABYAN   ANDY HAWKINS

JIMMY JONES   DALE POLLEY

JEFF ROBINSON   MIKE WITT

MIKE BLOWERS   JEFF NELSON

ALVARO ESPINOZA   GRAEME LLOYD

JIM WALEWANDER

Catching Up

```
N A G G I F E K I M I K E S T
O L D N H U B B Y C U B O N A
R L J A E S O L S I R K O R R
R E I O S R O L V A T S R E I
A L M V E O E T D E N E V Y M
N A M E E O P G N I B I D O S
Y T C Z S R U E B I L K O G E
R S I A R L E O G O C E N I K
R E N A D R R O E R B M Y B O
E Y T E G E Y O N L O D M R N
J B N D C E J R E K A J A I T
N B D U G D A R B O B B Y E T
C O R R A V A N R E N O I D A
T B A R E G D I W S I R H C M
N O S R E S T N A S Y N H O J
```

JORGE POSADA

BOBBY ESTALELLA

JOE OLIVER

MIKE FIGGA

DIONER NAVARRO

BRAD GULDEN

BRUCE ROBINSON

CHRIS WIDGER

TODD GREENE

TIM MCINTOSH

MATT NOKES

YOGI BERRA

JERRY NARRON

BOB GEREN

My Kingdom For a Starter

```
T R N O S R E T T A P F F E J
R E Y W A S K C I R G E N S T
O G R S L L I M N A L A S E H
Y M A N N H E R I M S A S R G
S G N U I N Y H Y T G S A Y I
Y I O S G O B A E E R Y U A R
L N R A O S T R L M I D M N B
V U L R N T A L A C N G E B M
E O A Y A I I Y O D N L T R A
Y E L R I H S B O B L E Y A H
O N R G N W G W R A T E K D R
Y A D W U D O E L A W E Y L E
F E A L R E G I R A L L I E G
T H C U C D E G T G E R V Y O
S A R O Y N A I L L U N O N R
```

SHAWN HILLEGAS
JEFF PATTERSON
ROGER HAMBRIGHT
NEIL ALLEN
RICK SAWYER
ED WHITSON

ALAN MILLS
GREG HARRIS
RYAN BRADLEY
BOB SHIRLEY
KEN CLAY

All Aces

```
P G E A R O S E N Y E U B T Y
M A B T C R N T R E A E T N L
A D U E T I E R H Z W U T I N
R S I L T I U D D E C H N R E
I O N R M C T A R Y M D O T D
A C E E S I V T E U Y O T D O
N Y H D M I R N E M F I N C O
O D O T D E O A C P T F A M G
R R A C I H L D B T Y S I Y T
I I O N K M A C E E I D O N H
V N M C N N S P R R L P N D G
E V I O I I Y E T E F L A A I
R R I E M D E L E A G S A E W
A Y L D N E D O O L C O N E D
S A M A R K L E I T E R R L Y
```

ROGER CLEMENS

RICK HONEYCUTT

ANDY PETTITTE

LEE SMITH

MARK LEITER

PAUL MIRABELLA

DWIGHT GOODEN

DAVID CONE

MARIANO RIVERA

RED RUFFING

ROD SCURRY

LINDY MCDANIEL

But Could He Hit a Curve?

```
N O D R A W E T E P Y D N A S
W N L G E O R G E S I M J P I
A T E S B N K I P B L U J S A
H E H E A O H O Y Z A C E T N
S M C A N G B U N N E U F T E
P S O A V I H W B O N K F U A
U T A I L A D E A Y M O M L C
L E R L K L R Y R T A F O K E
I V T T A N A I R T S J R Y G
C E C S H S G W Y R R O O E T
E A I A R I K L E M E G N K J
C D R O N D A R V K T K K C I
U D W E Z Y D N A R I I O I T
T B E N J A M I N M A M H M E
C E L E R I N O S A N C H E Z
```

JUAN BERNHARDT   MICKEY KLUTTS

MARK SALAS   JAY BUHNER

PETE WARD   BOB WATSON

BARRY EVANS   KERRY DINEEN

CECIL UPSHAW   MIKE WALLACE

CELERINO SANCHEZ   JEFF MORONKO

More Players

```
E D Y E K C I D L L I B E F R
Z Y E K C I D N O T T I G B A
O C L E T E B O Y E R L I N P
W J M N Y A L S H E A L Y A Y
A A E A A T N N T E L S A L H
L C R I C M O I S Y N K R L P
L K S H D O W B J E I I R Y R
Y Q M H A W I O K O E F U J U
P U I U F T H R B D B F M O M
I I T M E N I N L B I L E H Y
P N H S S A D O V E O K G N N
P N E O U V P R B J A B R S N
D T N I R A H A L E K N O O H
I C E Y T A L A E I O D E R O
B U G N U O Y H P L A R G O J
```

AL SHEALY

ED LOPAT

RALPH YOUNG

JOHNNY MURPHY

JACK QUINN

GEORGE MURRAY

AARON ROBINSON

BILL DICKEY

BILLY JOHNSON

BILL SKIFF

CLETE BOYER

ELMER SMITH

WALLY PIPP

Fighters

```
O T N E D Y K C U B O B J O N
N S R E D N A S N O I E D I S
E N R O Y W H I T E G N R L A
R O C E V T O I D U F J O T N
O T F I N M U D P L U K U S A
M L R T E O G R T A Z A T I T
R A N W N Y O O N A I V R L N
A W T A R R E B E L A D H L A
M Y H T N O O H E E S G S E S
O N U T K N T C H T Z O U N L
J N R S I E S I O I U E A H E
O A E L R V O R B Y R L H O A
S D L E R P Z U R C E S O J F
E A L W J A K E G I B B S D A
S I V A D N O R U H Y C I R R
```

JOSE CRUZ

LUTE BOONE

RICH BORDI

DALE BERRA

MATT KEOUGH

RON DAVIS

DANNY WALTON

JOHN ELLIS

RAFAEL SANTANA

DEION SANDERS

JUAN BONILLA

BUCKY DENT

OMAR MORENO

JAKE GIBBS

ROY WHITE

Tickets, Tickets

```
N E S S U A L C N O D N A R B
O P E G R O E G A N D E Y P D
S T N O S N A H Y R R A H U S
K D R A L E N D O N S O T H Y
C R L A M M C A L R I C R S S
U E E E G E I L A V H I T S E
K M N H I D L K I R N A L K N
Y A O E O H E O U P N R J C R
N T S N S V S E C B S A Z I A
N U A N E P T E A P U E E O B
H R N T A H I H V T I D S B E
O K S P E V N L C E I R D T S
J O U R A S T T C A T B F I S
O N A J E S R E F E N S D I E
Y F T N S E N R A B K N A R F
```

STEVE KARSAY   MIKE BUDDIE
DUTCH RUETHER   STAN BAHNSEN
HARRY HANSON   STEVE SHIELDS
RIP COLEMAN   JOHNNY KUCKS
BRANDON CLAUSSEN   FRANK BARNES

Another Puzzle

```
N O S R E D N E H Y E K C I R
A Y E N W O R B N I V E K L E
D R B D E L B R I S P E S L G
I U A H T I C A F H A R R E T
R N B H A S O F R H O I M W T
E O N O A R R A C B C T N O E
H P C W B M R U G K A A O P O
S C O T T B R A D L E Y R E R
T U H A D R R E H C I L R K R
A L A E O D M O S Y I O E A A
P A K D N P A B W Y B R W J C
G E C E S G U R E E S O D A S
N J R E I W T O W A R K T E O
I H Y O W S E P A M F F I L C
R I C K S O F T E R A P E T S
```

TOBY HARRAH   ROB GARDNER
SCOTT BRADLEY   CEDRIC DURST
OSCAR ROETTGER   RICK DEMPSEY
RICKEY HENDERSON   CLIFF MAPES
PAT SHERIDAN   KEVIN BROWN
JAKE POWELL

Show Me

```
R E D W A R R A M I R E Z C R
O E M A G N I S A L B E D A W
W R A M Z I G O J E N L W I L
L O J L A Z N I W H A L T R E
A L A O R T Y E M S Y T G E A
N A E H E O T V O E T K A D G
D N O R D G Y L A K S A R O D
O D C E R V I S A N K R E W I
F O H D B E T R M W C R Y F S
F F D O U W T I A A T E A I L
I F A S I T E T S R L O E M A
C I E C L E Y U L C D L N O P
E C K I R M H M H A L I E A T
R E L R E S I N O O W K C Y L
E S H E L L E Y D U N C A N E
```

RAWLY EASTWICK

SHELLEY DUNCAN

MATT LAWTON

WADE BLASINGAME

ERIC SODERHOLM

ROWLAND OFFICE

ROY SMALLEY

DAZZY VANCE

JOE GIRARDI

MARK KOENIG

WALT TERRELL

EDWAR RAMIREZ

All in the Game

```
E D R A L E V Y D N A R V O Y
A S E J E S A G O F E V I I D
N H K C I R R E F M O T L T D
O P C T N M E B E L I L C R I
L A O A D A M K H T J Y B E R
A S B G M G H Y L U W I F N P
C S R R E I D C R A T N L E Y
S I E E O N E G K E W E U G R
E L K T H N E H S N E T K A R
X E C A L S W P D A A S R D E
I V I G S M I O R E R R E U J
L Y N U A Y O F O I R O F Y C
E T K N U C O M Y D D F D O I
F I B O B W E K E A S D N H G
S N I L L O C T A P R A Y R A
```

RANDY VELARDE   FELIX ESCALONA
PAT COLLINS   FRED HEIMACH
B. (BILL) KNICKERBOCKER   RON WOODS
JERRY PRIDDY   FRANK CHANCE
JIMMY REESE   TOM FERRICK
CURT WALKER   RAY FISHER

Made the Yankee Blood

```
W S R E V I R Y E K C I M G C
F A T A R E C G M R E O S N H
I N Y S T W A I E K T C O I U
V I C U N R K C D T A S A R C
E R O P Y E N U O L R U N E K
H E N W H E K C H E A F I V Y
I D A E P E Y O D Y L E M E H
G R G S S R L N O A E T O R E
D A M I N L A T N R N N E E S
N I M E A K R I S E B O H V I
J S H N C H A R L E Y M P A Z
S O D I D Y O L T R V N O D A
M A R E E C N E P S A H O T M
D T H W O L B A B H F O R D H
T H G I R W N E K H O J O E P
```

RICK ANDERSON   JIM SPENCER
AL HOLLAND   GARY WARD
TOM BROOKENS   HENRY COTTO
JOHN MONTEFUSCO   DUKE SIMS
DAVE REVERING   MICKEY RIVERS
KEN WRIGHT   MIKE HEGAN

Way Back When

```
J O N A R E T S E H N O D I R
D O N H R E K A B K N A R F O
R A H D U O R V C T N C E R B
E R S N R C N I E L D E N A O
D D A D N N V A E I D U F N B
N E S M L Y W E L H O L F C W
A V I W M O M O G O R G E I I
X E L M E A N I R O D F H C L
E C A O G E H Y T B E R N O L
L S D E Y H N W E I Y B O B I
A O E E G D K E S R M B D U A
T V G U S O L A Y H L J B Z M
L I H A N A M F O H Y L L O S
A N T L K O S R S Y L O I L B
W G N I R D L O E B U R V B S
```

BILL REYNOLDS

ED SWEENEY

BOB WILLIAMS

BOBBY BROWN

SAMMY VICK

WALT ALEXANDER

FRANK BAKER

LEE MAGEE

SOLLY HOFMAN

RUBE OLDRING

DON HEFFNER

HUGH HIGH

With Yankee Pride

```
O W T N A R B L L A H S R A M
T D A R O Y S T A I G E R I N
F I N Y I V K R E L O T K I O
S E O R N F E L P A H E C A D
M R L S W E E G S E M A N R G
A E U G C D T Y A I O N O Y E
D V F R A A E O L V U H J F N
A E I H U L R O L O A D S I E
R S Y U G O S G O L C S O D L
E K B N M E H R R C E G N N A
C N E A V P E T E I Y S E O Y
N A B I L U L D A G M L O B D
E H C S O L T V P O E Z N E
P H A I N Y O K I T N R S A N
S C J O H N N Y L I N D E L L
```

MIKE MILOSEVICH

DON SAVAGE

SPENCER ADAMS

WAYNE TOLLESON

SKEETER SHELTON

MARSHALL BRANT

OSCAR GRIMES

HANK SEVEREID

GENE LAYDEN

ROGER SLAGLE

JOHNNY LINDELL

ROY STAIGER

They Wore the Uniform

```
B B E W T T E S S O G K C I D
S R I D N A S Y A R K O I E A
T O Y L M J O E M A H D S N N
Y Y L E L E O P N T V N T A I
E S A E L P R H E U O A A K J
N A K M T N I R N S H L R K O
N N S E A T A E N K O K D N H
E D U F V H E H R W N C I A N
K E J O U P O G M C L I N R N
Y R N D T J U T L I Y W G F Y
R S A K E S I N T A J L L H S
R D G I L M C D O U G A L D T
E G N I N N A D Y R R A H N U
J R O X Y W A L T E R S S U R
E K R I K L E S E G R O E G M
```

AL GETTEL
JOHNNY STURM
GIL MCDOUGALD
JIM HANLEY
JERRY KENNEY
ROY SANDERS
ROXY WALTERS

FRANK KANE
JOHN KNIGHT
AL WICKLAND
DICK GOSSETT
GEORGE SELKIRK
ERNIE JOHNSON
BILL PIERCY

Yankee Greetings, From…

```
P R O B I T O N U L I D G S M
E D D I E L E O N S E S O R Z
Z R N I E L E S N L E S O Z E
R O T O N H L S L T I L E E D
A T H Y T E A A E N L M F A N
M S R R K N L M R I O T R M A
I I A I S S I O E G R U E I N
D R M E T R A H Y A R M I J R
K H U O E R E T H S R Y S I E
I C N S A M F Y O C P H S R F
F L E N S E C R T P I E L Y K
F I D L L F H A R R Y R I N N
H T E O Z M O G L L I B M N A
W Y S L R S A R O M A R O O R
J I M R O L A N D E K N A R F
```

FRANK FERNANDEZ	EDDIE LEON
GARY THOMASSON	ROLLIE HEMSLEY
JIM RAY HART	DELL ALSTON
RICH HINTON	RUSS FORD
JIM ROLAND	LEFTY GOMEZ
EZRA MIDKIFF	

How Cool Were the Sixties?

```
R E R Y M E L T T O T S L E M
A Y H Y R O X K N C N T E S A
L E T G O N O E O L N E T T R
D L I O F E C D S A O V O E S
O A M T V M Y O T V J E L V H
W D S A E A B N O E O B L E A
N Y Y L I L B A L H H A I B L
I D E A L D O W L I N G T A L
N D L F L R B M I S M E O R B
G U R T O B L A T D E R F B R
O B A E J F R E D W R A L E I
J O H N N Y B L A N C H A R D
E H C E Y M L E H T O T S O G
F A C K Y D D U T B O B B Y E
F V I Y D E N N E K N H O J S
```

AL DOWNING

JOHNNY BLANCHARD

MARSHALL BRIDGES

THAD TILLOTSON

STEVE BARBER

MEL STOTTLEMYRE

BUDDY DALEY

JOHN KENNEDY

BOBBY COX

FRED TALBOT

CHARLEY SMITH

Our Outfielders

```
H K C I R D N E H Y E V R A H
L E P H I G E N L Y L E Y M O
R L R D U D Y T N A L O W R A
E N E S A N J V M L H I E R G
N R E Z C M O D E T E K X U N
N E R I T H Y K I L A N G S R
I N B N U R E R Y T D B K S E
K N K A C I A L I O R E O D B
S I C T L W R H M L P A B E E
P R I R E A W B Y A H A C R I
M O A N C E A Y O O R O Y R S
A H R Y V T L O W N R T A Y M
C F O E S E G D E O H L I G R
A R T O M M M Y D E R B O N O
V S I R O C H E L C A R T I N
```

HARVEY HENDRICK	CAMP SKINNER
MYRIL HOAG	ED LEVY
STEVE WHITAKER	NORM SIEBERN
CHARLIE KELLER	ROY CARLYLE
HERSCHEL MARTIN	RUSS DERRY
ROY HARTZELL	ED BARNEY

Only the Great Ones

```
D A V E W I N F I E L D A R L
R Y D R A W O H N O T S L E O
O L R G I R H E G U O L I N T
F G R O O C A L I B E O D O U
Y N E O G Y K T D N Y R A S Z
E I D U S E A N L N L F N S Z
T T D C K E R A E G E E T L I
I T O I G G A M I D E O J A R
H A S K N O K Y A K A J I U L
W M M L R O U E I R E N M G I
E N A Z N O Y K E F I D O H H
L O I U A T C C T W E S B T P
L D J E H T L I H P U O D E M
I J O H N N Y M I Z E C H R O
B O B B Y R I Z Z E L L A R T
```

ENOS SLAUGHTER

MICKEY MANTLE

ELSTON HOWARD

DON MATTINGLY

JOE DIMAGGIO

PHIL RIZZUTO

JOHNNY MIZE

ROGER MARIS

LOU GEHRIG

WHITEY FORD

DAVE WINFIELD

Outfielders

```
T S E I L P O L E R Y S T E D
J E S S E H I L L R I O Y K D
C H O W I E C A M P N H N O I
M A E P A U Q H E O T A G O G
Y N O B L Y U E J I L U X C N
S L J K O E T I C L H N I Y I
H A I U E R M M I H E G N T L
A R M A N D O M A R S A N S D
R M B M A Z C I U B W S F U O
R N I Y Y M O J Y H O M I D O
Y O K E M B U Q D N N R C T W
R M P R S I Y F F L N H W E E
I S O U V T I R Z A P H O Y N
C N H E C R C Y D I N G O J E
E E I W N A R E F D L A R E G
```

JIMMIE HALL   SAMMY BYRD
HARRY RICE   HOWIE CAMP
ARMANDO MARSANS   DUSTY COOKE
GENE WOODLING   NORM MCMILLAN
JOHN HUMMEL   JESSE HILL

Infielders

```
H A K I R B N U G S E C F E R
O A G C O E A A N E H T Y M O
P U R G I N T E G I V N G H N
A E A R L R F E C U A O G H T
L O Y I Y L R K C M D U Y R E
I W S L O W F E E A A E A W N
A T R R L E I L D P L Y O A I
T N D E W A O L N D M P M J C
O E D S K C N I L O U P E R K
R V T Y Y R K C R I A A N A E
O E L R C C A E M H A E L L T
R C R G E A H B C E G M R C T
G E U P A A R N Y S K F S Y E
J A R M R P E E H A C I L C N
P O P T B B A C Y L R A M S D
```

RAY MOREHART   CHICK FEWSTER
JERRY COLEMAN   JOE DUGAN
MIKE MCNALLY   RED ROLFE
ANDY CAREY   BEN CHAPMAN
R. (ROGER) PECKINPAUGH   CLAUD DERRICK
HARRY WILLIAMS   NICK ETTEN
RAY BARKER

Strictly Southpaws

```
T R E J I M L L I B O I C O N
H H N E O R H D F S A L M N A
S A O I G E R B S A I R E S G
T V R M K A P U E F K L T E E
Y R A R I S R A F G H T O K I
C O E G Y S W M G A H R E A D
T H E L U H E O M E G I V A R
S O E I L L A R R E M A S R A
J L R T T I O R C T Z E F I R
E A L O H H M L P U S M A Y I
M P N E T O A L K E W O G G G
R I U K W R F B L Y R T E U E
O G N T K D O F J I R L U O O
S A Y L W B E S O J B E N A J
H L L E R T T O C N G I S N E
```

BILL MILLER

ED WELLS

ENSIGN COTTRELL

GEORGE CLARK

HARRY HARPER

HANK THORMAHLEN

JOE OSTROWSKI

JOE PAGE

MARIUS RUSSO

JOE GIRARDI

BOB KUZAVA

CHET HOFF

Pick a Pitcher

```
T O T E L L U K E N E L S O N
R R Q T W I L C Y M O O R E T
E R U U I E A B O B L A L M K
T H U S B E H S D A L L K W A
N A D S S I B E M H A A O M T
E K P I N V L I I Y R S A L O
P A A O R E A L N L U H V E M
R R S H T E D N D O N M O N S
A L C G S E H R A O N R E G H
C R I E B O E S B T N R Y L E
B O N R J W L E Y O T O U Z E
O B A O S N I P M O N A V E H
B N E F S N F D A I R T L A A
D C G I R A E H S C E P S L N
A N T E R N I E B O R S H E A
```

JOHNNY ALLEN

ORAL HILDEBRAND

ERNIE BONHAM

SPEC SHEA

ED MONROE

LUKE NELSON

RUSS VAN ATTA

ROY SHERID

WILCY MOORE

KARL DREWS

BILL DONOVAN

TOM SHEEHAN

Here's a Mix

```
O R U S O N I E L S P E O N E
V H O R S E W O N A B D O O D
T I M L Y I L O U O I F N T M
N K C U L W V L R L E O Y A R
A A Y T A I Z A U B S K R L E
K O O L O U E P D T T C I L K
T E T H V R O Z R O U R P M R
R D I E R S M E E S D M U A A
S I L T N E B A L I A D J C P
E L H O H O H A T S D S I R Y
A C F C R S W S Y A C E R K A
O L N E O T M L A I X E R A L
A T N O O T L I N M S E E K C
F E I N A I E W T S E G H T O
G Y Y E B V R O N H A S S E Y
```

KIDDO DAVIS	ALFONSO PULIDO
GENE ROBERTSON	ROLLIE ZEIDER
KEITH SMITH	BILLY SAMPLE
RON HASSEY	VICTOR MATA
CURT BROWN	PAUL ZUVELLA
MARCUS LAWTON	CLAY PARKER

They Got Their Chance

```
N T E Y B E A H O W B L A T S
D O M R S R E I L Y L E H T H
L E S U N G I E K E I T W G A
E I L D A I Y A W E T X O R M
S X B P R P E D N O U L F I L
K E E E R A L K C F A P K N H
A O H Y N A H S R E I E R C S
J R W G C H T C Z U G S I M A
A C T Y U T Y T I A E K H O S
R H A D E H V G R R E G C E Y
E R D R I R H B L K Y V E O R
K N E C S T A T E D O B E R U
C V O R U R M K I D M R B N P
E T S I K E I A Y E N O A O W
R A H C I M R E R O K N R T B
```

BRIAN FISHER   KEITH HUGHES

MIKE GARBARK   DEL PRATT

JOE PAGE   MIKE KEKICH

RAY CALDWELL   ART DITMAR

BOBBY RICHARDSON   EVERETT SCOTT

ERNIE KRUEGER

Arms of the Men

```
Y U S T E V E H A M I L T O N
T N A E D N O S L O C D Y O L
O C I R N O R E L A B E S B B
R K D A A P N O A L L T R I O
I L A D L A R C Y V O N L L B
N M R A R G W N O D E L C L D
E O E C E R O I D O B Y R C A
V S U G B E G R E U P E A A V
E R E E M T A T R I N E D S I
S O R R U H A B E R I S R T D
K F B G C F A H U A L Y E R S
N R V I N C E T H I E K S O O
A N R O H N M A I L L I W A N
R E A R O I L O Y D C A L T O
F H M T J A C K W A R H O P P
```

BILL BURBACH	LOYD COLSON
JOHN CUMBERLAND	MARV BREUER
RICHARD DOTSON	JIM TURNER
BOB DAVIDSON	GREG CADARET
STEVE HAMILTON	DON COOPER
JACK WARHOP	CY PIEH
BILL CASTRO	

After the Strike Year

```
M E T Y R R E B Y A M N H O J
N Z O R E O R E H L A Y L T C
R O E V A U D R L M I E R U N
T O L U D G S N G F E U R E O
R H G Y G B E E E M T T L A S
U E M E T I T N A Y K B L B B
L A V S R S R Z Y A S L E A O
Y L E E E E Z D U W E C J Y H
G U E V W I R F O C H I O H H
K T A W L N M I A R M C W T C
E D M L O A A P C L N N T O T
D I I O N H N F E K Y I T U U
O E L E H H Y W E A S U W L B
R L A A O T I A L T E O D D Y
N I W J I S H A J E S T N M E
```

DAVE STEGMAN
LEE MAZZILLI
BUTCH WYNEGAR
BUTCH HOBSON
EDWIN RODRIGUEZ
JOHN PACELLA
ROGER ERICKSON

RODNEY SCOTT
JOHN MAYBERRY
RUDY MAY
JAY HOWELL
STEFAN WEVER
JIM LEWIS

The Latin American Connection

```
F U R Z E R I M A R R A W D E
J U A N E S T R E N O Z O A N
R U T E S O J A L U W O E U J
I P A L D S O O D R O T O P L
C A P N O E H R L T N L M E E
O S A J E R O E I A A B U D O
H C L I O S F U U E C O N R H
N U A O N R P G P A R B E O E
I A R E D H O I O L U B Z C R
Z L E E J I L F N N E Y I O N
E P Z H L E L D O O Z R O N A
R E T I F O T E R I Z A R C N
O R C U O L A Y T T A M L R D
V E N T I M O G L I A O C E E
C Z O J E R U N E M U S I N Z
```

CECILIO GUANTE   LEO HERNANDEZ

JUAN ESPINO   FELIPE ALOU

BOBBY RAMOS   MATTY ALOU

F. (FERNANDO) GONZALEZ ED FIGUEROA

PASCUAL PEREZ   EDWAR RAMIREZ

Before the Radar Gun

```
G L O N N I P H I L J O N E Y
M N L K A W Y A H E I O S N W
F I R E A G Y B N A J U Y A F
E C K T S X R R L D E L K U O
N K J E W S Y O E M L Z S A B
D C A B C B U C M E U E O Y W
U U K B Y A R R W M L H K V S
S L E M C I N E N K O S A O A
P L M X R G L T C E K T M L N
O O I A U L J U W Y L F K M Y
T P D I M T B A H E W L N C T
M N A E T S I Z E F L N A V N
E P L H S I E D V I O L R U E
D C E E S T O B E N A Z F G A
L E J I M F O R G E S T I H V
```

JESS BUCKLES   MIKE CANTWELL
ALLEN RUSSELL   CLEM LLEWELLYN
TOM MORGAN   TOMMY BYRNE
NICK CULLOP   FRANK MAKOSKY

How Was Their Throwing Arm?

```
B I N O S K C A J E I G G E R
D R U G H B E R T R A M A K E
L J O S R E D N A S N O I E D
E C U N I H I M J F R N E T D
I A H A S B B I U D V E O A O
F Y E A N O M A D Y N N H O J
N W L E D B N A G M Y D A N U
I R Y T K C E S R T A B R Y A
W U F J R N U N A K S O R R N
E B F E A E I R I R W B T I R
V U U K L V A W T Q D A Y A I
A K G I U S I M O I U I L L V
D S T L C R K E I T S E N C E
Y N N O P W M K Z R E C Z H R
L L U B A T R A T Y N N A D A
```

DEION SANDERS   JOHNNY DAMON
BRONSON SARDINHA   CHAD CURTIS
DANNY TARTABULL   JUAN RIVERA
TONY TARASCO   REGGIE JACKSON
JUAN BENIQUEZ   DAVE WINFIELD

Racking Up the Wins

```
G R A Z N A M L A S O L R A C
N O P U T A P E V C E C I L G
N J I M K O N S T A N T Y I R
O C W H A S T O O Y O A V D A
D I O Y U D O F J I E R J A D
R N W B J N E S R A L N O D Y
A E A G N U M J B O E M E P H
E V X L N A Y C O X T I N F I
R E G N I R H E O B N A I R B
F E U J N E S L W L O K E O J
F Y S V U K E C T A M B K I V
E H D J Z E W V F E H K R O T
J D M O L I E K A H C A O Z Y
T E P O S L L E W D I V A D L
S D S R E L H O W K R A M F H
```

JOE NIEKRO

BRIAN BOEHRINGER

RICH MONTELEONE

CARLOS ALMANZAR

DON LARSEN

DAVID WELLS

DAVE EILAND

BOB OJEDA

JEFF REARDON

MARK WOHLERS

JIM KONSTANTY

Guarding Those Groundballs

```
D N N A M U A B Y D D A P O T
L A H G U M P E R S E V D C A
T E N T R O B E C C A M L H D
W Y A G R E L L E S A K U A S
J I E T E E B L L H W I A R E
P E K L S L W M A O B M P L L
A L F O N S O S O R I A N O T
T C J F F A H J I L S L B K T
K I O O M E T A I N B A O A E
E N M U R A N R R M N N B H N
L O H R I D N E A I E E O W G
L R I L O N I T T U S N D R I
Y L E Y G A U V O Y N R E G A
L H L P O Y S M I T W K E Z R
R E S P I L L I H P Y D N A G
```

PAT KELLY   PADDY BAUMANN

D'ANGELO JIMENEZ   JEFF MANTO

ALFONSO SORIANO   ANDY PHILLIPS

GRAIG NETTLES   BRIAN DOYLE

DENNIS WERTH   RON BLOMBERG

```
K E N J E C A L L A W E K I M
A E Z B I R G A E S T R Y B A
T D L Z O M D L A O P G O E V
N R Y L T B W L H R U B S R C
O A W I Y I B A C R B T R U M
S L T O F S R Y I Y E T R A I
L E S R N I T Y M V O T E S K
I V E A U S M I E U B N K T E
W Y R N O C T H N L R D I I G
G D O J S C O J E N M C C G A
I N G A H W E F G U E I E N L
A A E E E O A T W E N T J R L
R R L N P R W O G N I K T O E
C L G E Y R A E L M I T E Y G
E D A R T S E D S E T S E R O
```

MIKE GALLEGO   J. T. SNOW

STEVE HOWE   KELLY STINNETT

ORESTES DESTRADE   BOBBY MITCHELL

GENE MICHAEL   CURT BLEFARY

BOBBY MURCER   TIM LEARY

JIM LEYRITZ   RANDY VELARDE

MIKE WALLACE   CRAIG WILSON

Names of All Nations

```
T N A P A G R O M D W L E Z T
C U S E N O J L Y R R A D E L
E J C T P E R A N A Z W R D U
S U N E J S Y M D U E R J N A
E O I I K L H P R T Y E U A O
N A S N T L Y C D M R D A N L
O W U C E K N E U U H N N R L
S A H A A A O L S R E A P E I
T G I V V R H W O M M V A H N
R I F I P O A T S A O N D N A
E I D G L M T Z J K R H I A Z
N E U L K A E K O O I O L I N
I K A I C P I R O C F J L R A
E N B A P L U C Y S A I O D M
D E T N O M L A K C I R E A J
```

J. (JOSIAS) MANZANILLO

TERRY MULHOLLAND

JOHN VANDER WAL

D. (DARRELL) EINERTSON

ADRIAN HERNANDEZ

C. J. NITKOWSKI

OSCAR AZOCAR

ERICK ALMONTE

KEI IGAWA

PETE INCAVIGLIA

IVAN CRUZ

DARRYL JONES

JUAN PADILLA

Some of Mr. Steinbrenner's Boys

```
N D T O A J O S H P H E L P S
I A R H N T V C J A S O N H C
A R T A G A I M T O R C Y I K
L R C M P I V O R R O W U L I
R E K R A P N A I T S I R H C
E L A L E T I K P E T A S U G
B L S Y E W T L N L B S L G M
M R A W B M O D C O R O E H T
A A B I M S A R E R D A Y E E
H S S P O I O R B S E N C S L
C N I E C O M G U M A L A H L
A E R O N S A T G D I L Y R I
B R H U O I L W M A N J V T B
O A C T I A N I L O M E S O J
J C H R I S J A M D I O R N E
```

BRANDON KNIGHT

CHRIS BASAK

CHRISTIAN PARKER

MATT DE SALVO

JOSE MOLINA

JOSH PHELPS

DARRELL RASNER

CARL PAVANO

JOBA CHAMBERLAIN

PHIL HUGHES

TYLER CLIPPARD

JIM BROWER

At the Ol' Ballgame

```
D N N D R E W S K A R I T F Y
M O A O N C E N I A N O R R H
I S Y E L Y R R E T L O B E E
E U N L G N U O Y L D E N D N
N N I O E S U M F N R L O B R
T G L J S A I R E N L T S E Y
K A U I T N L L I E O I B E R
I M H M A R H E W O N D O N O
E M E Y E O A O X H I O D E D
W I K M S L G Y J A F D T N R
I J R S L Y E M A K N H A S I
C G O E R O S S K E C D P E G
Z R N R E D Y P E R O I E L U
O N A S A F L A S O I L N R E
A L B E R T O G O N Z A L E Z
```

ROSS OHLENDORF

ALBERTO GONZALEZ

HENRY RODRIGUEZ

D. (DOUG) MIENTKIEWICZ

DOYLE ALEXANDER

JIM MAGNUSON

TERRY LEY

FRED BEENE

NICK JOHNSON

SAL FASANO

LARRY GOWELL

PAT DOBSON

BERNIE ALLEN

Are You Old Enough To Remember?

```
J A C K T C K E B U K Y N O T
E R D S I R R U B Y A R S O N
O S T A N W I L L I A M S N S
M H S T O M U N D E R W O O D
N S O R O E C O L N E S M S Z
O N M S E C E M E H R I A N N
T I A G C M S B R E K T N H I
N S R T I S H E T E D G R O L
I Z O P E R R E G O R A M J L
L R R A T A P R O R Y F F F I
C R D M H Z I H C B O E C F H
U O E W T F N I U G N E R I P
O L P I F O L R S U A E G L S
L R R I D F N O H I P E L C D
I F N O C S N O T N I L C U L
```

LEN BOEHMER
ROGER REPOZ
FRITZ PETERSON
TOM UNDERWOOD
MIKE GRIFFIN
RAY BURRIS
GEORGE SCOTT

PEDRO RAMOS
PHIL LINZ
STAN WILLIAMS
LOU CLINTON
DON HOOD
CLIFF JOHNSON
TONY KUBEK

Just Give Them Some Wheaties and a Resin Bag

```
J W S S E D O N S T I T U N M
T E A E D R A E Y B A Y T H C
M O F Y S L A N H A E R H A Y
A O D F N M E P N E L E R P B
E R R D J E I I L Y V C L I G
P O D T W O F S H E R I N G A
W B A O S I H R J S R I O E B
A M N O E Y L N A B E W O N K
I C T X A N B L S N O V I S I
L D R A R S Z Y I O K H E T J
L O E D P L E E T A N L V T B
I N W N G S E N N R M O I N S
G A R Y J O N E S T A S T N G
M L E P N E C T R A M M E L H
S D Y H I R B S T R A A O V E
```

TODD WILLIAMS   JEFF JOHNSON
WAYNE FRANKLIN   ROB MCDONALD
DANNY RIOS   STEVE SHIELDS
GARY JONES   KEN CLAY
MARTY BYSTROM

Outlaws of the Outfield

```
R U B E N R I V E R A N D L E
E J E R O B E R T O K E L L Y
C E K D A R Y L B O S T O N E
N S I A L U E R B A Y B B O B
E S M A I L L I W D L A R E G
P E I I R C I M O H T N A H G
S B K Y K T R E O O U R K E A
E A E N R E D A N N H O J N R
N R J N V I A Y G O D O E G B
A F A I O T W L H M L E T H N
H I L R S O B U D O I U S R E
S E S B M I K E O R T R A I R
O L I A B R E U P S E H A P R
N D C S E N I A R M I T E K A
E K N O S N H O J E C N E L D
```

GERALD WILLIAMS   PAUL O'NEILL
JESSE BARFIELD   ROBERTO KELLY
SHANE SPENCER   BOBBY ABREU
KARIM GARCIA   RAUL MONDESI
DARREN BRAGG   TIM RAINES
TONY WOMACK   MIKE ALDRETE
RUBEN RIVERA   DARYL BOSTON

Here's a Staff For You

```
S O F Y C M A E B J T F S N K
O T R O Y S I N R A R C E Y A
L C E S W E A K S T O B L L D
S L T C N J N A E T J E I R L
V I H A H E R U T M F S E O D
Y P D T V E T E R A Y N Y E M
T E H N V I R S R B S E N R H
R U L E E I O N R A N O R T Y
O T S D C Y S D R A L A I S N
A O I K I W P L O L K M I A N
J N S A O L L O I T S F I R E
K O A R P E Y V N T E T F K B
N E T O R N N R T S R L O E H
L H L A D O V A O B O I S C J
I W D S R F M E R C A N R C S
```

OCTAVIO DOTEL
SIDNEY PONSON
DARRELL RASNER
KYLE FARNSWORTH
SCOTT ERICKSON
BRIAN BRUNEY
RON VILLONE

CORY LIDLE
JOSE VERAS
JEFF KARSTENS
MIKE MYERS
T. J. BEAM
MATT SMITH

'98 Meant 114 Wins

```
C A W U S N D A C M B O B B Y
H P S I G S A A I I D T E B O
U E W E P I O K L K D U C J C
C T O E M G E D H E E F O G I
K E Z S K L J L R J S A B J H
K E N E O S O I L E Y V A O A
N D R W D M U H W R D Y E V L
O E E I U N L R N Z T D D U J
B L P L T F A E B E K X O I M
L Y P A S U B N S M R I Y T J
A K U T Y C P S R B I R A X E
U C T E R A M M S E R J A M O
C I E N O E O E V C H N K D F
H R Z I R O Y R E K L O E I F
S U I S O R B T T O C S U K Y
```

JIM BRUSKE   JAY TESSMER

MIKE JERZEMBECK   TODD ERDOS

DARREN HOLMES   MIKE LOWELL

SCOTT BROSIUS   DALE SVEUM

CHUCK KNOBLAUCH   RICKY LEDEE

O. (ORLANDO) HERNANDEZ

Here's What 200 Million-Plus Got Us

```
T O M G O R D O N I R T S E R
R A Z E N P U D G N S O A N G
I V O I C I Y M N T I N O G N
A J N F P O D E T A V S O M A
S A S O R O H D K R R A A U W
E E R Y S N N M E E L R K G G
E Z V O A N E A D R K I X A N
R A E E N R H N V B M W U L I
B H S C I S A O E A U I A B M
M X P C H N M L J C P J T H N
E T O W O D L A U Y T L F E E
N I N S U H E I L K D I R B I
A G A E O D R U W L D N O A H
L J U R Y A M L L E R R A D C
A B N I L T E C E M I G G R U
```

JASON ANDERSON

DARRELL MAY

RANDY JOHNSON

CHEIN-MING WANG

CARL PAVANO

WIL NIEVES

TOM GORDON

TIM REDDING

SEAN HENN

ALAN EMBREE

MARK BELLHORN

AARON SMALL

MELKY CABRERA

Did You Get His Autograph?

```
O L L I T S A C O T R E B L A
G S R Y J O E K I L N O J R R
K A G E K T I L T M I O E M U
R S R Z G U H O U B H Z C A T
A S O Y E N O G M N T E L T N
L O T U S N I A O R C E E R E
C F O W F H I L U I X Z O O V
Y Y P A I G E T L A R L N S N
N N I D N R S F R E Y A A T I
O O C O U N I I F A B E T U B
T T S D O E A P B I M Y S W O
E A E Y L S R N O M E O A Y R
J H N D F T O U S I L L N L E
K A E G Y D E C E I Z A D I C
T R O N D E L L W H I T E B T
```

TANYON STURTZE   JOHN OLERUD

TONY CLARK   GARY SHEFFIELD

RONDELL WHITE   DON BAYLOR

ALEX ARIAS   TONY FOSSAS

ALBERTO CASTILLO   JASON GIAMBI

ROBIN VENTURA   CLAY BELLINGER

TINO MARTINEZ   CECIL FIELDER

Broadway Boys

```
M S Y E L S M I R G N O S A J
I D I H Y H P R U M B O R E K
K J S R O S S T L S U C N O W
K O L D E F H W I J L R O R M
E N A E C N I V B S O U I H Y
V L W G Y V A O T B N C I A U
I I T E P D B P S S K I R F E
N E R A S M O O M Y M R X A S
B B E S E D N M B A U E B O R
R E U L H A Y O T M C E D O N
O R V O V M N T E R U T A V E
W I T O A E L L N I U R R E T
N S N R S U A C O N T R P E A
N O G I K D O F E R A L I H B
D L S E M A H T S U C R A M Y
```

JASON GRIMSLEY
BERT CAMPANERIS
MATT LUKE
RUSS DAVIS
JON LIEBER
DONOVAN OSBORNE

DALE MURRAY
RICKY BONES
BOB MELVIN
ROB MURPHY
KEVIN BROWN
MARCUS THAMES

More Pitching Pleasures

```
L A I K S W E L S A W Y R A G
Y G E S H A N E R A W L E Y N
N R D R E E F B E L W A R C I
N E V U K O L G O U V R I L L
M T I E T R O Y B B E R C S O
C N C T H C M W L P G J O E J
G U R H D T H O D Y I R V W O
L H A E E N O R E C K C I R H
O H S R I W O D U P E R N M N
T S C R V L E I S E E Y A Y N
H I H H Y P N T T U T R M P Y
E F I A W L P K A C K H R A S
N T G R A S C C I H T S E Y A
B A N A R F S I N N H O J R I
E C L L E W O D C M M A S D N
```

SPARKY LYLE

DUTCH RUETHER

BOB GRIM

DICK TIDROW

LYNN MCGLOTHEN

SHANE RAWLEY

GARY WASLEWSKI

VIC RASCHI

JOHNNY SAIN

SAM MCDOWELL

CATFISH HUNTER

GAYLORD PERRY

RICK CERONE

They Had the Glove

```
Y R T S T E V E B A L B O N I
T A E I S A N D Y A L O M A R
T O L Y M E L R A H C I B L E
O Y N M S F R A D D N I B E Z
G A O A B A O N U N L C O R Z
N U O T L U C L O L N E B V A
A G Y B F L D F Y R A L N Y L
P A B G E N E M I C H A E L Y
M S W E I S A Z E T R K R G N
O I E V P R C E A T T F I S O
C U R I T K A D S G H O E U T
T L Z I T A N E V I E E L M L
O E N O I L O F M I T K N E O
D N S U S E J E D N A V I Y M
R I S Z E U G I R D O R A M I
```

SANDY ALOMAR

STEVE BALBONI

TIM FOLI

GENE MICHAEL

IVAN DEJESUS

BILLY MARTIN

BUD METHENY

LYN LARY

TONY LAZZERI

MIKE GAZELLA

A. (AURELIO) RODRIGUEZ

LUIS AGUAYO

We Saw Them in the '70s

```
A D L E I F T I H W Y R R E T
N A S M A I L L I W T L A W O
Z E N I T R A M Y P P I T A M
N J I O D N A R U E P L L M A
A G G I S E N D I X B L N L L
M R G G T N O S L E E R L A A
G A O E A D H O B I I E R A R
R M C R E T S O N O N S R P R
E O H E U Q B I J I R U I O Y
B C C B R O P K P X G B L L M
E I I L L U G U D Y E C E A U
V R R I O K O I R O F L A Y R
A N V L O L E R U M E V A D R
D E T S I K A D U S L L I B A
R O B E R L R O N G U I D R Y
```

LARRY GURA   BILL SUDAKIS

WALT WILLIAMS   TIPPY MARTINEZ

TERRY WHITFIELD   LOU PINIELLA

RON GUIDRY   LARRY MURRAY

ALEX JOHNSON   DAVE BERGMAN

RICH COGGINS   BOB OLIVER

A Million Fans Saw 'Em in the '20s

```
S A M M Y T O S E A L D N E W
T I M S N I L L O C P I R L A
O S K I D N E L S O F A L L L
R L R S K N A I R A R E D T L
E H E E E W M K D H E S O Y
G C V S G W U S F C V I O U S
I N E W U O A G T O G L W L C
Y E L I A E R I R K H I C N H
E R A N H E M M T M T D H A A
C F D K Y Y E B O E A M E S N
U Y E B N R D P O T H L O R G
L A U N O R T R E B A O Y C F
E R H T O R O G G A R B Y K H
O O L Y L L E N N O C M O T E
J A N I P U X I M Y N N H O J
```

RIP COLLINS   RAY FRENCH
JOE LUCEY   BOB MEUSEL
BRAGGO ROTH   TOM CONNELLY
WAITE HOYT   TOM ROGERS
AL DEVORMER   FRED HOFMANN
JOHNNY MITCHELL   WALLY SCHANG

Picture These Players

```
D I M M O M A Y F O R T J E C
O K U E I D O B G N I P T H S
T C D A K E L S O H T N I W C
T V D B V C K E W F O C E T I
E I Y L U C O N J E K R N I A
R J R I J M T I E E N J O C N
R E U Z U D P A N E B O O G W
E R E F O L O H G U L S B R O
T A L U O R A Y A T I E E O R
S D Z N D W R E B D J P T E B
H N E K K V U K N S L A U J O
C O I S X A N N C O X E L A B
T F U T H E O I R S Y J Y T M
U O W E K I M H G E F I R T U
D R E D O S A R E W E I L U J
```

CHICKEN HAWKS

PING BODIE

DUTCH STERRETT

HINKEY HAINES

JULIE WERA

JUMBO BROWN

LUTE BOONE

BUMP HADLEY

LIZ FUNK

MUDDY RUEL

Mound Men

```
W L S A R G P I P E G R O E G
A A L V E I R C W A R E T B J
M I L E I U R T A F Y J O O M
A L K T B C G S I E B B W S A
H T E S S P T O K L T I A R R
T D L R E M M W H U G U P E T
E A R E D L A A R Y I E K D Y
F S O I Y H E L C O B C T N M
U N O W S D E V L E I B R A C
R Y W B I Y O N O W I E O C H
T H O D I N E N P C O H D B A
P B I K U L Y M A N N O C L L
O T C R G B E G A L O A D R E
A A F E O K E C E V D J T O A
F N I R E G N I L R E R T S R
```

KEMP WICKER   MARTY MCHALE
GEORGE PIPGRAS   BOBBY HOGUE
STAN COVELESKI   ATLEY DONALD
ARCHIE CAMPBELL   BOB TURLEY
WALT SMALLWOOD   BOB SHAWKEY

"H" Is For Hurlers

```
I  B  Y  W  O  R  O  B  K  N  A  H  C  I  S
G  L  E  N  N  A  L  T  R  U  C  A  K  Y  T
H  N  D  U  F  I  N  N  E  R  A  N  E  L  A
A  A  A  R  N  O  S  N  H  O  J  K  N  A  H
L  Y  R  R  Y  C  A  F  F  O  M  R  P  R  A
L  P  T  R  E  B  L  U  D  A  P  O  T  I  L
A  I  L  H  Y  N  Y  W  W  O  R  B  L  E  M
N  H  E  S  I  W  N  R  N  O  R  I  U  W  O
I  R  S  I  L  I  E  I  R  E  E  N  S  Y  R
E  W  N  M  O  T  D  N  F  A  K  S  S  E  R
R  O  R  E  U  F  R  A  G  Y  H  O  E  R  O
E  R  O  N  O  S  N  I  L  O  P  N  R  G  W
S  E  J  N  E  K  C  I  R  T  A  P  T  N  O
O  H  I  P  O  L  I  T  O  P  E  N  A  Y  W
N  R  E  H  C  A  M  U  H  C  S  L  A  H  Y
```

HIPOLITO PENA   HARRY BYRD
HANK BOROWY   HANK JOHNSON
HAPPY FINNERAN   HANK ROBINSON
HAL LANIER

Pitch and Catch

```
B D A G I Y L A E H N A R F T
R I O F N R R N T O M E R S E
N T D N O A S R A L N Y K I G
E O R C S D L Z E N O C X R N
S Y B U K L O N I B I C E C H
L I A A C E A K I R O B A T J
E X O R I N S U D G M E O O E
I E L U R L E N G A U Y K Z F
N R O H E U E R D H S I T I F
T E A O R H M A E I T V N B M
T A J J E W R E W G N A C G G
O T S I G B K R L U B R I I A
C O L A O C H S Y A R O I W C
S L I B R T U T O L D Y B A V
E K N O S D U H S E L R A H C
```

ROGER ERICKSON

DON SLAUGHT

DALE MURRAY

CHARLES HUDSON

SCOTT NIELSEN

FRAN HEALY

ELLIE HENDRICKS

MIKE O'BERRY

JOEL SKINNER

BOB GEREN

Now Batting….

```
J H A N K B A U E R C Y R U W
O O G E R A R T F I X E U L I
H R L U E R G O D Y I D S A L
N A E R O J H W R V N O T L S
N L M D R G Y D A V J T Y E O
Y U S H L K N J I Y A N T E N
O N E T Y E N E O X N A O R D
A Z L E H A I A B E O E R A E
T O L M T D T F M Y R R R E L
E O I S P I N T L O N O E K G
S T B I W A U N Z I T N S A A
Y M R L A O H R A S C T E L D
O I L D R O E I V A J E O B O
B K E L J O H N N Y H A C K S
N O S R E D N E H Y E K C I R
```

RUSTY TORRES   JOHNNY OATES
STAN JAVIER   TIM HENDRYX
RICKEY HENDERSON   HAM HYATT
BENNY BENGOUGH   CECIL FIELDER
WILSON DELGADO   HANK BAUER

Can't Go Wrong With the Right-Handers

```
N O T T A B O B B Y M U N O Z
U S I A T A H C N W A H S E O
B D R O V I G L E N N H D A O
A G H E N R O Y W E A N L R D
R U E I H I D S E W A I E R E
I J R C E T A O N N O V S I V
I N O V I D A C R U A O D L E
K W E A R L H E Z E T S E H C
E I B J R A H F W I E S E M A
D L E E C R I F T D V T L I N
I T Y O E E F U G H I S S B A
H E N I S E R M I N O V I C U
S O V R J P Y G L A T K A U J
W A N I S S U M E K I M R D L
X E L O E L R T R E N C E R E
```

JUAN ACEVEDO

MIKE MUSSINA

XAVIER HERNANDEZ

HIDEKI IRABU

SHAWN CHACON

AL REYES

DAVID WEATHERS

BOBBY MUNOZ

LUIS VIZCAINO

JEFF WEAVER

Ever See Them Spit?

```
C H A L O B A E S T T O C S C
U S U B I C A R K E M M I C K
L A M N L F A E C C A H H O A
T M I A E F O B I N T R S T M
E M K D I E R E S Y I F D T Y
N A E S I L L A A S H G O P B
R R T E V O L S T O W N A R S
E S H R A C T I I K A D L O O
M O U B N L A R W V Z L E C R
O N R I C N N O Y E A N S T C
O E M D S E A U A O I R I O A
C K A E F G Y N J P I N T R B
N U N A M A R G X E L A R C B
O T R E T S L E N I V E K E U
R O N O S N E H W E R D T E B
```

MIKE THURMAN   ALEX GRAMAN

TRAVIS LEE   RON COOMER

SCOTT SEABOL   JAY WITASICK

SAM MARSONEK   DREW HENSON

KEVIN ELSTER   BERNIE WILLIAMS

BUBBA CROSBY   SCOTT PROCTOR

C. (CLAY) CHRISTIANSEN

Clemens Got #300 With

```
C H R I S L A T H A M A R T S
U I C C U L L E D D I V A D T
R D F I L E C I M N A D N J A
T E Z E U P G Y J O H O R O N
I K N E L S I T Y L M T E S W
S I I T E I N R L M I B D E O
P M R I A Y X E A R I C K C E
R A P L E T I H W E B A G O T
I T T A N D S A E W I T H N M
D S E S M I U L Y R O D I T U
E U R E R T M F L S E G S R S
O I B H R J B N F O F D O E I
M N C T E U E H R M E L I R C
A G O C S O R O E S S E J A J
R E H N I T A J C A K I L S G
```

JOHN FLAHERTY

HIDEKI MATSUI

JOSE CONTRERAS

GABE WHITE

CHRIS LATHAM

CURTIS PRIDE

DAVID DELLUCCI

JESSE OROSCO

FELIX HEREDIA

CHRIS HAMMOND

BRET PRINZ

DAN MICELI

On Deck

```
L N B A C F R I C H A R K E R
E B I O A N R A I J O V A C E
O G I T B S R A M K S Y U R V
J E R L A B N O N A E T P E I
U O K E L E Y E B K L V O I L
T O E R I M L S G L B L I N O
E O N S A F C Y H R I A L A B
N N M O E L O K O A O W K I O
I G E G S W C S E D N J D E B
V O N R O T E E T C N T T E R
E R U V O R A L C R H A Z R T
R E M D K N M W L A E N I I A
E W D I A N V A B I R H I R L
T O B L L G E R N O N O R E B
S O S T A H S E I O B E H M L
```

TED WILBORN

FRANK BAKER

BOBBY SHANTZ

IRV NOREN

BILL MCKECHNIE

BOB OLIVER

BILL LAMAR

BOB WATSON

HORACE CLARKE

BRIAN DOYLE

TOM GORMAN

JOE SEWELL

ART JORGENS

Fan Favorites

```
J N O T F O L Y N N E K P U D
O Y E L T H O M I T U E K A O
E R O A C I H I F T T C I T N
P L B E W R M J T E I R O O A
E Y T E O C Y S M W A I S M L
P D G T N I S I T L A N C M O
I N O E I V K S E O G A A Y R
T A H S I K A D C B D O R H U
O R T I E E N S U N S D G E P
N I S L Y A O O S O R U A N I
E T S L C K U S R M E J M R M
O E W N Y H C R A L N S B I D
N A H D O G N I V L A K L C G
R O N A S D F O R I V G E H A
J A Z I R O J I M B O U T O N
```

KENNY LOFTON

PETE MIKKELSEN

BILL MONBOUQUETTE

JOHN CANDELARIA

OSCAR GAMBLE

TIM STODDARD

JOE PEPITONE

JIM BOUTON

TOMMY HENRICH

ANDY KOSCO

RAWLY EASTWICK

RON KITTLE

Yankee Types

```
E N I G A N R O T E E Y R A G
S I L R K N A K O L U K E T E
C V A C A C S E M C L A N U N
G O B L M T O E Y O M A T N S
O E K A L B R N T A V U I R L
R T O C B M Y I N I E U S E A
B D E R I E D B D E Q G S O T
S H R L G E D R B C P I N M U
I R L A R E U A M O A B B A N
D E A A W T B E H M T A R R R
R T M E S N G U Z L I S E E O
A R P M S R O T R R G K T E H
L S O W O N I R E N A R E D C
Y T T E E R E C A O S G E A I
R I G E F S A K E A T O Y N V
```

TOM STURDIVANT   FRITZ MAISEL

KEN SEARS   HERB PENNOCK

BABE DAHLGREN   GEORGE BURNS

GEORGE MCQUINN   AARON WARD

ELMER MILLER

Putting On a Show

```
B E W U J O N E S P R I S G Y
V S Y A R R I K H O V E O R U
R O T M Y J E I Y K R O Y A N
I I C T A N L T E O S R B N S
S C C D E N E N E E B N E L A
O T O K I S B G G J A J R U K
N P E E R R O R M K R D R E
K H K V E H S O Z A K E L T B
Y R O T E S O T D Y N O R H A
O A T J A T L D L N K G O E R
M K I G Y O R Y E L A D E N D
A G E I H M L O L N D I C R G
T O D N H E M T U L T A R I U
T T E S R E W O A T W H L B O
U K J I M K A A T L E I N A D
```

GOOSE GOSSAGE

KEN HOLTZMAN

RICK RHODEN

DOUG DRABEK

BRIAN DORSETT

WAYNE GRANGER

KEN BRETT

PHIL NIEKRO

STEVE TROUT

TOMMY JOHN

DEREK JETER

JIM KAAT

The Year Was 1977

```
H O O D L T A S I V A D N O R
E T A Z A I T M B I D G E D U
R X I A T V T E S R E P E Y P
D N O M I J E L L O G N X L A
A O J D S C C R R L N D N A U
L I M O D R R G A I U O P J L
B H T I E A E A S J O G I G L
N U T D N Z M S G T S M N W I
I F N A E G H T S O B I L O N
L A Y B E E O U T E S E C O D
L M E D R H I R A O M A H H B
U R L R K B E T A E I Y M V L
A K I C C A T K U M B L D A A
P L O B O I L D I V O D L N D
L A S V E B U G L M I S B E A
```

ELLIOTT MADDOX

GEORGE ZEBER

DENNIS SHERRILL

DAVE RAJSICH

ANDY MESSERSMITH

DAMASO GARCIA

JIM BEATTIE

DOMINGO RAMOS

MIKE HEATH

DON GULLETT

PAUL LINDBLAD

RON DAVIS

Remember?

```
Y G E L D N A R N E L K M S B
P N A L P T K O L B J A O G E
S E O J E S I D A R U F R I W
C W A S H I N G T O N A T R I
A N R A I A C K Y O N V S A T
S E S E R L A H L T U R Y D A
E K O N T R L J J U B E B R L
Y I E G M A S A I W V X Y E O
C L K R A L C K C A J O T N V
O A F T E K S Y H Y H T R H N
X R L A S I T A N E N S A R I
O F R O M E G A S N O N M T S
G E N U S N O M E B A B H O K
R E R E L D U H X E R D C O A
T D D E N O T S N H O J Y A J
```

LEN RANDLE   DANNY CATER
JACK CLARK   MARTY BYSTROM
C. (CLAUDELL) WASHINGTON   CASEY COX
JOHNNY CALLISON   REX HUDLER
JAY JOHNSTONE   GRANT JACKSON

It's a World Wide Game

```
I  N  S  S  I  L  U  M  A  T  O  T  I  V  I
R  G  O  K  E  I  G  T  H  L  O  N  T  K  J
E  M  U  D  A  V  E  P  A  V  L  A  S  O  I
V  R  O  S  O  O  T  A  N  D  O  W  E  L  M
A  A  I  N  N  N  H  C  M  E  O  L  N  U  M
G  V  V  T  K  I  E  A  C  B  E  W  A  O  Y
Z  O  E  O  N  D  A  O  A  F  I  V  P  D  D
T  T  S  T  U  B  U  R  E  I  J  E  U  O  E
L  R  O  S  C  A  G  B  H  N  Y  D  Z  Y  S
A  A  F  T  E  Y  V  V  I  O  Y  A  S  T  H
S  S  E  C  N  R  H  N  R  E  S  T  P  F  O
K  E  T  N  E  A  R  N  E  D  L  O  F  E  N
C  C  H  I  E  R  D  H  U  H  E  N  I  L  G
A  O  R  H  E  C  T  O  R  L  O  P  E  Z  A
J  G  E  O  R  G  E  J  O  S  E  R  I  J  O
```

MONK DUBIEL	GUS NIARHOS
LEFTY O'DOUL	HECTOR LOPEZ
JOHNNY GRABOWSKI	VITO TAMULIS
JOHNNY BROACA	JIMMY DESHONG
JACK SALTZGAVER	CESAR TOVAR
JOE LEFEBVRE	JOSE RIJO
DAVE PAVLAS	

A Mix of Outfielders

```
R O T W I X E N H O L D E R Y
Y O V D A V E C O L L I N S A
A E Y D A I Y M M I J G I S L
Y G R W R L X O N E V E R J L
Y E V H E A B N A I T I A R T
Z N L E P A B K E L P C J I T
S E A D O M T M C A K I N A E
I L L N A S U H O I M O S L Y
R O H E I R O M E L R T E B A
R C T A V D B J Y R L F R L D
O K A R O O E T D R L I H U N
M L C E H N T H T I R Y H A A
L E L Y S L I T O O I E I P I
A A R E E D O T O M C N J G R
H R N D E W L E B N U S G O B
```

PAUL BLAIR
JACKIE JENSEN
ROY WEATHERLY
DAVE COLLINS
JERRY MUMPHREY
GENE LOCKLEAR
RICK BLADT

JIM LYTTLE
OTTO VELEZ
HAL MORRIS
PHIL LOMBARD
SCOTT BRADLEY
BRIAN DAYETT

Call Them a Right-Hand Man

```
T O M B U S K E Y I N L G E D
S D P R J I C O E O L O D S O
H T R R W O T U C I R R A A M
H M E A N L E C I D F L A M I
D E A V H G O V O N E R Y J N
R T R N E N N E X A D S O O
O Y N B K S R I F R A V N N R
F D E T M H U E T R B A O E L
N G O L O C R N B A G A F S A
A O W D R G Q L D R E P N T M
S T E A U U A U O R E K W I I
D S H S C E T M A L A T Y R C
E E O D N A M B K I E K L A R
R N I O R O Y D O C D R I A R
F I G E T D E J E B C L A M W
```

WALTER BERNHARDT   ALEX FERGUSON

SAM JONES   NEAL BRADY

FRED SANFORD   RAY KEATING

HERB MCQUAID   STEVE SUNDRA

TOM MORGAN   BOB TURLEY

GORDON RHODES   ED KLEPFER

JOE VERBANIC   TOM BUSKEY

Who's On First?

```
M O S G O O D A R R Y I N D Y
A B A E H D T E C Y M A N M A
R U I W G O N D I G M A A R J
V D S L I N R D T E R R I O A
T D U L L A Y I E H V N K F C
H Y N O R S H E M T E S S B K
R H E B S A K R H M I T O E S
O A S N I L L O C E O J H E P
N S W O Y K R B W E D I Y L I
E S I D K N E I S R T R R A T
B E L A B S P N N E O E K D G
E T L E H O E S O L F N K C E
R T R M S L T O T W I G C H R
R R A M A V O N R O G A I M I
Y O T E B Y K S W O R K D O R
```

MARV THRONEBERRY   BILL SKOWRON
EDDIE ROBINSON   JOE COLLINS
DON BOLLWEG   BUDDY HASSETT
DICK KRYHOSKI

```
N I T I P P Y M A R T I N E Z
D N A H K S E E I N E D T Y E
A S O G O R A C M P X T T D M
V A C S U L H A T O A H O N A
E M A I D H U L N M G T R A G
P M R R I O L L R I A S U L N
A C O N Y V O A R O C N E O I
G D T O R E Y W A S K C I R S
A O H N W O N E K B G E I M A
N W V A I E S K O C I P N I L
O E X R K N K I N F I G O J B
W L F F G C Y M A R G D S W E
E L L E W O G Y R R A L F O D
C I R E T A L B E V E T S T A
M I K S W O K M I L K N O R W
```

DAVE PAGAN   RICK SAWYER
MIKE WALLACE   STEVE BLATERIC
LARRY GOWELL   RICH HINTON
RON KLIMKOWSKI   JIM ROLAND
TIPPY MARTINEZ

Strike Year

```
T  R  N  O  S  R  E  T  T  A  P  E  K  I  M
N  O  E  D  U  C  N  E  W  I  S  T  A  R  R
O  I  B  T  Y  D  A  L  M  I  J  G  I  I  D
S  T  O  I  O  T  G  R  E  A  S  C  O  C  R
T  T  W  A  H  O  I  W  C  N  K  A  E  K  O
R  E  I  Z  A  R  F  E  G  R  O  E  G  R  F
E  H  C  U  L  S  F  Y  E  N  E  S  E  E  H
B  G  H  R  E  I  A  U  R  G  B  T  N  U  S
O  I  R  E  M  N  G  L  A  R  F  L  E  S  A
R  R  I  M  I  C  C  H  U  C  A  E  N  C  R
E  E  S  A  H  A  M  I  K  E  L  B  E  H  E
R  V  O  E  L  D  Y  R  O  A  G  E  L  E  K
D  A  L  E  V  A  D  H  T  I  I  K  S  L  C
N  D  U  P  U  R  N  T  S  I  E  P  O  A  U
A  D  A  V  E  L  A  R  O  C  H  E  N  G  T
```

DAVE RIGHETTI	GEORGE FRAZIER
ANDY MCGAFFIGAN	MIKE PATTERSON
DAVE LAROCHE	GENE NELSON
ANDRE ROBERTSON	RICK REUSCHEL
TUCKER ASHFORD	BARRY FOOTE

Let's Not Forget

```
D J B O B T E W K S B U R Y F
I E O O S T N E M E L C T A P
E B N E B E W C I H R A I S I
P L A N B S D A K F E B L O E
O E S W I N H Y E O M M Y Q R
C L T H L S O I A T O S N U E
S L C E L E R Y R R I H K I H
A L L S F K T A M L N C G N A
R L A P U I N S S W E A S B S
A E R E L R L O T M N Y L Y B
T T E R T O F S R E U E I L U
Y I V I O A D S O N Y S M I S
N H O F N O R T N N U O S D S
O W E Y B Y E R G V A H U E E
T B I L L G U L L I C K S O N
```

BILL GULLICKSON
DENNIS RASMUSSEN
BOB TEWKSBURY
MIKE ARMSTRONG
TONY TARASCO

BOB SHIRLEY
PAT CLEMENTS
PETE FILSON
BILL FULTON
ED YARNALL

Final Innings of Puzzles

```
E U P W I T S R K N O W A M O
F A C J M D E S O P T T O C S
M O Z N E A A E L E D T G S N
P I F O T F R N I Z R M E A W
A L K R D L F K N E D S C I Y
U L R E F N G J W A R N L A E
L I L T S I E E U H U L C M L
G D C E H T R M A D I L I O N
I T R D N B A N O E E T T R A
B T E H Y W D N B R Y N E Y T
S R B L N Y A A T I I A H N S
O N L A F I N T L O T M T S E
N I G O R K S O S K N O A M K
B U X A S R D W R O N B H R I
D O M I N G O J E A N I R A M
```

WILLIE BANKS   MIKE STANTON

SCOTT POSE   MARK WHITEN

MARIANO DUNCAN   MIKE STANLEY

RAMIRO MENDOZA   ANDY FOX

PAUL GIBSON   DOMINGO JEAN

BILLY BREWER   ALLEN WATSON

DAN NAULTY   JEFF JUDEN

No Clark Kents Here

```
S C O U R B E S O V I W E L R
V A H N H E I D E G E R E S O
U M Y U I S K U L Y R R E P G
T I T E C I E E L O B K N E E
I K M C K K E S N H I N M J D
N E A O A J C H O P A A P A H
C M N R T L A A S M H K V Z O
L C N A C N O E R C Y E K Z M
L C Y O S R I R A Y L R L A C
I O L E D L E E M A O N R P I
B R N E R H M I P Y J A S E S
O M S A D B J O M A L Y E O J
M I H E O W I I S M P L E P O
A C E B E N J A C K O R E G W
Y K Z I T A U Q S A P N A D E
```

JERRY MOSES

ED HERRMANN

MIKE MCCORMICK

CHUCK CARY

DAN PASQUA

BOB MEACHAM

CHARLIE SPIKES

DAVE LAPOINT

RON HANSEN

KEN PHELPS

JIM YORK

Fun Names

```
K S E N R A B Y E N O H I G N
C A N I L B U M P H A D L E Y
A J D E O L R U Q E P A S W I
B N U K L T A S I B W P H E S
N E N S D U S H F N U I O B I
I O V A S A E K L D T L G V L
A H Y O M I E M C E M C A T L
T I V S L U E H Y E M L E C E
S M M I U M A W E E B R P X K
K E I S S N I B N T L N R E C
C V J J D T O L Y R I S N N O
U A I L T Y O H S D I H N I D
T B E N Z U C K E D D T W E Z
T R U C K H A N N A H A S B H
R E K C O H S N A B R U P S F
```

HONEY BARNES

S. (SNUFFY) STIRNWEISS

SPUD CHANDLER

ZINN BECK

SLIM LOVE

HENSLEY MEULENS

PADDY BAUMANN

TUCK STAINBACK

BUMP HADLEY

TRUCK HANNAH

WHITEY WITT

URBAN SHOCKER

MEL HALL

DOCK ELLIS

Not Just Any Ol' Joe

```
N E L U F D R O K A T S E O J
J O E C O N T S E M A J E O J
O I J O E G E N D J O O R O O
E T O J J A C K O E D E E Y E
S H E Y O R L E B A R G R E B
M A G E E E G U B B O D O H U
I R L O G L S J A R J O O S R
C R E J E H W M D C O W M E T
H A B N D O E O I N E S E L H
O Y N I E J N O C T R I O G O
U R U D O J O E J E H K J E F
Y E O J N A P T E O O R E O I
A I K S W O R O B E O J T J E
T O S H E O N T A I C A N A O
S I R R O O M I R R O G E O J
```

JOE COWLEY   JOE GORDON
JOE GEDEON   JOE GLENN
JOE SMITH   JOE BUSH
JOE BOROWSKI

Call Me a Yankee

```
M H I G S B O B B Y B O N D S
I I A K N U R O D O F F I L C
J R K R U I Y A K T R A D E B
Y I T E R A R E D I E O E U T
E C M A M Y C E O G D R D A O
N L R L N O S F V R U D T W M
N I A S E A R I U E Y L S P R
I F P T I W D G M H R E D A E
K F S I C W I C A P M E M E N
C M A B R E E S M N S A V I N
M A G E A R S L D Y L O P A T
H R D D U E I V M L D A N L D
C K O E T S E N L I E N B V L
I L R T O F F I L C J H U R E
R E N S R U B E N S I E R R A
```

DAVE REVERING
JIM LEWIS
BUDDY HASSETT
BILL LAMAR
RUBEN SIERRA
RICH MCKINNEY

MIKE MORGAN
CLIFF MARKLE
HARRY SIMPSON
BOBBY BONDS
BRAD GULDEN

Victory Is Essential

```
Z Y T T H G I R W T E R A J A
Z E T I N E B O D N A M R A A
P C D A N I E L O W E R A N L
E I O N E B O O L I S E I V U
T S M L A H B D Y V O S D E A
O I E O T N C G E F S C R N P
I O R E O E R A S U J O A T E
N T E R R R R E M U T I P A D
A N A V J N G B H N R U S M E
S A P O I U I Y E L O D U I G
U L S T I N M V D A E N R G R
A V C G O V E E E D N H I L O
E I N T Y K O R F K U R C O J
O O N T I K C S S I L B L I I
J A C M E C O L T E R B E A M
```

MICHEL HERNANDEZ

JORGE DE PAULA

ARMANDO BENITEZ

JARET WRIGHT

KEVIN REESE

JOE AUSANIO

AARON BOONE

BUDDY GROOM

CHARLES GIPSON

COLTER BEAN

MIKE VENTO

New Millenium Men

```
H A L R A N D Y C H O A T E N
R C T R C L C B O P F D E A O
J A L A A H L R E E E C W R S
O A E L W N R E L N I J Y O R
E S K Y I F D I N T F A N V E
W G C E E H X Y S W N O A E D
E N O B W J N U K T A W R L N
S A P L O E J H E U T J D E
I R C S A D S O L Y I R S U C
E T E G I R M T P L E S N O O
S Y L V O P S Y B B A M L E N
T E A N S A L N I R Y N E E R
O D L O S A N P H I O L E S R
R A N Y L L I L D E T O P L H
O N I A C Z I V E S O J K S G
```

GLENALLEN HILL

JAKE WESTBROOK

ALLEN WATSON

CHRIS TURNER

RANDY KEISLER

FELIX JOSE

RANDY CHOATE

DAVID JUSTICE

RYAN THOMPSON

JOSE VIZCAINO

TED LILLY

BEN FORD

What Gamers

```
F R E D S T A N L E Y W J O E
I S E G T N A P E K T A O R H
L O D K T D O A U E S L I A D
Y M R L R J M S R L O C L U E
N A R U O A I A B I S L P W D
N O V O H N D M A O E F J A J
E C S U G A Y Y D B D E N O O
K E A T C E T E A E R T E W C
G T Y G I B R R R R I C A I Y
I U E S K H I S Y E O D S P P
N R L E O M W L L L I C E K D
G J I L L D U D L A G L J L N
U O M U I M O I E U G J L T I
P L A W P C N V E V I L O A W
Y P R E O S A T N O R I E L D
```

FRED STANLEY

PAT DOBSON

GREG CADARET

ERIC SODERHOLM

PAUL MIRABELLA

ALLIE REYNOLDS

ED WHITSON

JIM DEIDEL

ROGER SLAGLE

B Is For Baseball

```
E B O B C H A P T U C K I N G
L B E A C O N L U B U R O C A
I O N R B I L O H T R O B R B
V B S O T A D I E K I N L B B
E C T A S D R B I L W B I U Y
T I C F J N A T H O B L B C O
N V L D A R I N R B L T B K U
A V R E C B O B I H S G Y Y T
E S J L T W Y L O E O B D D A
I N N A K B L L B R L I N E B
L E S B B Y D O F B E S O N C
R B K O R E B G O B B C B T A
A T B A N U B A B E Y O U N G
H E B O M U R E O N I P A R T
C O F F O L S N E W H C T U B
```

BERT DANIELS   BILL HOLDEN
BOBBY BROWN   BOB CERV
BRUCE ROBINSON   BUCKY DENT
BUTCH WENSLOFF

It's a World-Wide Game

```
G E R M A N Y S C H A E F E R
X F I A M L A M L A M N A C H
U O R K E F B H D I G O M A A
A H O E S N R O C F R B A M L
L L S R D E F A L S H A U M S
L V L L A H L I N Y V B L I C
A E U L A M E E I A T U U R H
M S L H A W A I V T K Q O G U
A K O M C I Y N M O R U B E M
L I A F A S T M E A C S C R A
M U A B Y N L E M B C N Y M K
X O L R A C E M R I U H A A E
A C R A B J I B L O J R M T R
M E K C A J E V U O C N A T S
J I M I K S O H Y R K K C I D
```

JIM MARQUIS   FRED HEIMACH
RUBEN AMARO   JIMMY WALSH
STAN COVELESKI   AL MAMAUX
GERMANY SCHAEFER   DICK KRYHOSKI

```
C Y Z E U Q Z A V R E I V A J
E A H R Y A N F I L O F D C P
S Z A T U E S O L N A A H A P
I C E A R P S L N P N R U A M
R U O U L A I L D N I L U O R
R O N T G R C O A S Y L N D U
A A D A T I N C C H Q L O R T
H L L R U B R H M U D Y O B S
E L D L A A A D A E H A G N Y
O E O Y E M U N O W O E R I N
J I L N B I T Q K R E J D B N
L O A L B R T A L H X B H D H
R A I N I R I E L U E E I O O
E S H L A R R I R S A A L L J
S O L L I R T N A U Q P D A L
```

SCOTT BANKHEAD   JOE HARRIS
CHRIS CHAMBLISS   JOHNNY STURM
JOE MCCARTHY   AL LEITER
PAUL QUANTRILL   JAVIER VAZQUEZ
ALEX RODRIGUEZ   BRAD HALSEY

Lumber "Jacks"

```
J A C K R A K E R K C A J E C
J A C K C A L F U E R R U R O
N A C K O F O U R T U J E C D
E J C L L J K C A B M I K E J
J C A K L J A J J A N J W K A
K A L C I E A C A R A O J C C
C J F A K E W C U C D N A A K
A A R C A B J O K C K J C J J
J C A K B L F E D M A C K A A
O J A C K K N O N C A A C C C
F K B A C R W A K S M R A B K
K C J A I E C A C K E K T L S
C A J G W C K A C K J N C I O
A A H E N E B A J W C G I A N
J T D E R I R H C C A J O R J
```

JACKIE JENSEN

JACK AKER

JACK FOURNIER

JACK ENRIGHT

JACK MARTIN

JACK MCDOWELL

Searching For a Hitter

```
S A V E H C I E L G K N A R F
E L B M A G R A C S O T S E R
N K I O L E N E R O N I A K E
O D E D L A X I M A V C C C G
J E R N A E R D M A R A R I N
T W I O N P O K D E J E A N C
R A R S I Y N I C P X A T E R
E G A Y E I L R N H L N S O I
P N J A R I U O U V E A V R N
P O P B H M T D F A R V R Y O
U L D C Y E L N A T S D E R F
R E N B I E K O O I O M E A L
C I B S R U B V M A R N J G E
A O S T O J A M I E Q U I R K
B L O G E R U M B P L A T S Y
```

KENNY LOFTON

REX HUDLER

BOBBY MURCER

CHILI DAVIS

GARY ROENICKE

FRED STANLEY

JAMIE QUIRK

OSCAR GAMBLE

ED BRINKMAN

RUPPERT JONES

FRANK GLEICH

HAL LANIER

They Had an Experience

```
D L A N O D C M L L E Z N O D
I I I Z N E B E A R Y P C W B
X V R L A G U V O T L H O R Z
I T A O G I D E N D A N E E U
E H L C R S O M A D S T H T P
W C E A O B T L C I T C H M S
A H D T M I O U N J N G C O L
L I N H E F R T O A I U B R T
K P A R K T A D S R B G H O W
E U C U I N I Y N N W A A C U
R R N S M E E E I D E A T E H
N C H A D R K U B L G K R S D
D O O T N C I K O R W R O D E
A S J H A R R Y R I C E O L N
M H I J O S E C A N S E C O A
```

DONZELL MCDONALD	REY SANCHEZ
ROBINSON CANO	CHAD CURTIS
JOHN CANDELARIA	JOSE CANSECO
JACK ENRIGHT	BOTS NEKOLA
BRETT JODIE	HARRY RICE
MIKE MORGAN	DIXIE WALKER

Absolutely Yankee

```
L E E N U T T M F I V E A L I
T Y R N U N O S L I W S I R K
A S N E O T O D D Z E I L E E
I H G A R S O T E D L A E H S
B C L S M M R S R L I B O T A
B I O S P R A A A O O X E S D
R D L M A E E C E B B V I R P
I E C L T L C T M P E E E E D
A M H Y B M V C T K E W B R K
N C A R Y U G A A E H T I A E
D O O R T R R R P E U B N E B
O D R O A N S B N E G G G O I
Y A M W D A R S A U V A E H M
L S K C Y O O U O C L A C E L
E C H T A N W D F T H U D E L
```

LEE GUETTERMAN

BABE BORTON

DREW HENSON

DOC MEDICH

DOUG BIRD

BOB MCGRAW

BRIAN DOYLE

BILL BURBACH

LARRY MCCALL

MONTE PEARSON

DAVE PAVLAS

KRIS WILSON

TODD ZEILE

The One and Only

```
B A B E E B A B H T R B A B E
A A A B U R E A B A R U T B B
B H B A B U T B B R U T A H A
B T E E A T T E A U T R H B B
H T R U B H U R R T B A B E Y
T U R E B A R U T H U B A T T
U R H B E B A B A E R U U B U
B E H T A A R U A U H R R A R
R B T T U B U T T B Y T H B B
U B U T U R A H R B R T U U H
B A R H E B E B A B U U R A T
A B E B E R U B B R E E B B E
E B A B B U U R A A B A B A B
B B B B A T R A B B E A B A A
R U T H B A B E H U R E T A B
```

BABE RUTH

Nothing to Bobble With

```
T R A Z I A O L N A B E T S E
I O R L E S T O N G C P U R S
G R S E L T T E N G I A R G T
C S R E O F P O K I K C J A A
R U E E Y D R A D E S K F R B
A E R E W R Y O Y M M I J Y V
I R E T N O S B O D T A P G E
G A H O K C R T B D E D H I O
D Y E L D A R B T T O C S A F
I Z E N M E U G B C B P U R E
N I L C O S I F A O L N D C H
G R A I G C U R M T B A E O L
M O M A R E G O T A L U A P S
A I J E L G A E N Y N N E D S
N R A S O R A S O R Y D D U B
```

BOB BROWER
PAT DOBSON
CRAIG DINGMAN
ESTEBAN LOAIZA
SCOTT BRADLEY

BUDDY ROSAR
GRAIG NETTLES
CURT KAUFMAN
DENNY NEAGLE

Plus These Guys

```
Y A N A N A T K N A R F A R B
S E T E V I N C I E T R I R D
E S M I R U M D A B O C A I U
N J H E D N D C O T D N E M T
U A A Y O T A A R E D H A L C
L R M C E N Z M E O T T L L H
T E E E K L Y Z E N T M O I R
T V K K L P I G Y L O B W K U
A I L S U O O A A V O P M R E
M L A F T L C W B B E C A E T
O O T R M U T P E F B N P V H
M B R Y D O T T I L F E A I E
R O E K N E H C A R L E T N R
A B N A N A D N O M R A J O C
C I M F E C N A V Y Z Z A D E
```

RIP COLEMAN

DUTCH RUETHER

FRANK TANANA

JACK POWELL

BOB OLIVER

DAZZY VANCE

MATT LAWTON

MATT LUKE

Hitters Anonymous

```
E N A G B O R T A O E C M H R
R A U L M O N D E S I D O E S
H I E H R U N O A N I S T S R
I V E E Y N I S R T E S I O E
L R X T H H O R E S I V N P L
S M Y E T C P C E E L L E A L
I H S O O F O R M T L U C U U
M E A I L S H R U S I H O I C
T S D N O A H E A M W M N N C
U R O F F E T O T L B C A L M
O W S E W I U D H E E O L A E
G H L E A R T A G A H V R T C
I N V R I C Y M T I M G A F N
V A E U B D A L Y L C D U D A
D T D A V E L A R O G N T A L
```

LANCE MCCULLERS   RAUL MONDESI
DAVE WEHRMEISTER   ROB MURPHY
DAVE LAROCHE

The Fat Lady Sings

```
W P K E L L L Y G R A S M U T
N A T E S I K E R L R B O C Y
D U L A N N O U D V O E R N E
N L O L N N E J D I B A B O K
A A M T Y A Y A I R E S E W Y
L S T A N W N R L M R D O R M
E S I O T A H A O H T R M S M
T E O O M T S I T G E P J T I
T N N C N M H U T K E A U L J
E M A R K I Y O A E N R T U K
W A L B E R G J W E H A S O S
N C H A R L Y A O A O U R P N
H H S E L B R O F H R J R F I
O E M O P L A S Y I N D I S R
J R E B A S M O J A L H A P R
```

MATT HOWARD   KENNY ROGERS
WALLY WHITEHURST   NEAL HEATON
PAUL ASSENMACHER   FRANK TANANA
JOHN WETTELAND   JIMMY KEY

New York Yankees All-Time Roster

A

Jim Abbott
Harry Ables
Bobby Abreu
Juan Acevedo
Spencer Adams
Doc Adkins
Steve Adkins
Luis Aguayo
Jack Aker
Mike Aldrete
Doyle Alexander
Walt Alexander
Johnny Allen
Neil Allen
Bernie Allen
Carlos Almanzar
Erick Almonte
Sandy Alomar, Sr.
Felipe Alou
Matty Alou
Dell Alston
Rubén Amaro, Sr.
Jason Anderson
John Anderson
Rick Anderson
Ivy Andrews
Pete Appleton
Angel Aragon
Rugger Ardizoia
Alex Arias
Mike Armstrong
Brad Arnsberg
Luis Arroyo
Tucker Ashford
Paul Assenmacher
Joe Ausanio
Jimmy Austin
Chick Autry
Oscar Azócar

B

Loren Babe
Stan Bahnsen
Bill Bailey
Brad Baisley
Frank Baker
Steve Balboni
Neal Ball
Scott Bankhead

Willie Banks
Steve Barber
Jesse Barfield
Cy Barger
Ray Barker
Frank Barnes
Honey Barnes
Ed Barney
Chris Basak
George Batten
Tim Battle
Hank Bauer
Paddy Baumann
Don Baylor
Walter Beall
T. J. Beam
Colter Bean
Jim Beattie
Rich Beck
Zinn Beck
Fred Beene
Joe Beggs
Rudy Bell
Zeke Bella
Mark Bellhorn
Clay Bellinger
Benny Bengough
Juan Beníquez
Armando Benítez
Lou Berberet
Dave Bergman
Walter Bernhardt
Juan Bernhardt
Yogi Berra
Dale Berra
Wilson Betemit
Bill Bevens
Monte Beville
Harry Billiard
Doug Bird
Ewell Blackwell
Rick Bladt
Paul Blair
Walter Blair
Johnny Blanchard
Gil Blanco
Wade Blasingame
Steve Blateric
Gary Blaylock
Curt Blefary
Elmer Bliss
Ron Blomberg

Mike Blowers
Eddie Bockman
Ping Bodie
Len Boehmer
Brian Boehringer
Wade Boggs
Don Bollweg
Bobby Bonds
Ricky Bones
Tiny Bonham
Juan Bonilla
Lute Boone
Aaron Boone
Frenchy Bordagaray
Rich Bordi
Joe Borowski
Hank Borowy
Babe Borton
Daryl Boston
Jim Bouton
Clete Boyer
Ryan Bradley
Scott Bradley
Neal Brady
Darren Bragg
Ralph Branca
Norm Branch
Marshall Brant
Garland Braxton
Don Brennan
Jim Brenneman
Ken Brett
Marv Breuer
Billy Brewer
Fritz Brickell
Jim Brideweser
Marshall Bridges
Kary Bridges
Harry Bright
Ed Brinkman
Chris Britton
Johnny Broaca
Lew Brockett
Jim Bronstad
Tom Brookens
Scott Brosius
Jim Brower
Bob Brower
Boardwalk Brown
Bobby Brown
Curt Brown
Hal Brown
Jumbo Brown
Kevin Brown
Brian Bruney
Jim Bruske

Billy Bryan
Jess Buckles
Mike Buddie
Jay Buhner
Bill Burbach
Lew Burdette
Tim Burke
George Burns
Alex Burr
Ray Burris
Homer Bush
Joe Bush
Tom Buskey
Ralph Buxton
Joe Buzas
Harry Byrd
Sammy Byrd
Tommy Byrne
Marty Bystrom

C

Melky Cabrera
Greg Cadaret
Miguel Cairo
Ray Caldwell
Charlie Caldwell
Johnny Callison
Howie Camp
Bert Campaneris
Archie Campbell
John Candelaria
Andy Cannizaro
Robinson Canó
José Canseco
Mike Cantwell
Andy Carey
Roy Carlyle
Duke Carmel
Bubba Carpenter
Dick Carroll
Ownie Carroll
Tom Carroll
Matt Carson
Chuck Cary
Hugh Casey
Alberto Castillo
Roy Castleton
Bill Castro
Danny Cater
Rick Cerone
Bob Cerv
Shawn Chacón
Joba Chamberlain
Chris Chambliss
Frank Chance

Spud Chandler
Les Channell
Darrin Chapin
Ben Chapman
Mike Chartak
Hal Chase
Angel Chavez
Jack Chesbro
Randy Choate
Clay Christiansen
Al Cicotte
Allie Clark
George Clark
Jack Clark
Tony Clark
Horace Clarke
Walter Clarkson
Brandon Claussen
Ken Clay
Roger Clemens
Pat Clements
Tex Clevenger
Lou Clinton
Tyler Clippard
Al Closter
Andy Coakley
Jim Coates
Jim Cockman
Rich Coggins
Rocky Colavito
King Cole
Rip Coleman
Jerry Coleman
Curt Coleman
Michael Coleman
Rip Collins
Pat Collins
Joe Collins
Orth Collins
Dave Collins
Frank Colman
Loyd Colson
Earle Combs
David Cone
Tom Connelly
Joe Connor
Wid Conroy
José Contreras
Andy Cook
Doc Cook
Dusty Cooke
Ron Coomer
Phil Cooney
Johnny Cooney
Guy Cooper
Don Cooper

Dan Costello
Henry Cotto
Ensign Cottrell
Clint Courtney
Ernie Courtney
Stan Coveleski
Billy Cowan
Joe Cowley
Casey Cox
J. B. Cox
Bobby Cox
Birdie Cree
Lou Criger
Herb Crompton
Bubba Crosby
Frankie Crosetti
Ivan Cruz
José Cruz
Jack Cullen
Roy Cullenbine
Nick Cullop
John Cumberland
Jim Curry
Fred Curtis
Chad Curtis

D

Babe Dahlgren
Bud Daley
Tom Daley
Johnny Damon
Bert Daniels
Bob Davidson
Chili Davis
George Davis
Kiddo Davis
Lefty Davis
Ron Davis
Russ Davis
Brian Dayett
John Deering
Jim Deidel
Iván DeJesús
Frank Delahanty
Wilson Delgado
Bobby Del Greco
David Dellucci
Jim Delsing
Joe DeMaestri
Ray Demmitt
Rick Dempsey
Bucky Dent
Jorge DePaula
Claud Derrick
Russ Derry

Matt DeSalvo
Jim Deshaies
Jimmie Deshong
Orestes Destrade
Charlie Devens
Al DeVormer
Joe DiMaggio
Bill Dickey
Murry Dickson
Kerry Dineen
Craig Dingman
Art Ditmar
Sonny Dixon
Pat Dobson
Cozy Dolan
Atley Donald
Bill Donovan
Mike Donovan
Brian Dorsett
Octavio Dotel
Richard Dotson
Patsy Dougherty
John Dowd
Al Downing
Slow Joe Doyle
Jack Doyle
Brian Doyle
Doug Drabek
Bill Drescher
Karl Drews
Monk Dubiel
Joe Dugan
Mariano Duncan
Shelley Duncan
Ryne Duren
Leo Durocher
Cedric Durst

E

Mike Easler
Rawly Eastwick
Foster Edwards
Doc Edwards
Robert Eenhoorn
Dave Eiland
Darrell Einertson
Kid Elberfeld
Gene Elliott
Dock Ellis
John Ellis
Kevin Elster
Red Embree
Alan Embree
Clyde Engle
Jack Enright

Todd Erdos
Roger Erickson
Scott Erickson
Félix Escalona
Juan Espino
Álvaro Espinoza
Bobby Estalella
Nick Etten
Barry Evans

F

Charlie Fallon
Kyle Farnsworth
Steve Farr
Doc Farrell
Sal Fasano
Alex Ferguson
Frank Fernandez
Tony Fernández
Mike Ferraro
Wes Ferrell
Tom Ferrick
Chick Fewster
Cecil Fielder
Mike Figga
Ed Figueroa
Pete Filson
Happy Finneran
Mike Fischlin
Brian Fisher
Gus Fisher
Ray Fisher
Mike Fitzgerald
John Flaherty
Tim Foli
Ray Fontenot
Barry Foote
Russ Ford
Whitey Ford
Ben Ford
Tony Fossas
Eddie Foster
Jack Fournier
Andy Fox
Ray Francis
Wayne Franklin
George Frazier
Mark Freeman
Ray French
Lonny Frey
Bob Friend
John Frill
Bill Fulton
Dave Fultz
Liz Funk

G

Gabe Gabler
Joe Gallagher
Mike Gallego
Oscar Gamble
John Ganzel
Mike Garbark
Dámaso García
Karim García
Luis A Garcia
Billy Gardner
Earle Gardner
Rob Gardner
Shawn Garrett
Ned Garvin
Milt Gaston
Mike Gazella
Joe Gedeon
Lou Gehrig
Bob Geren
Al Gettel
Jason Giambi
Joe Giard
Jake Gibbs
Sam Gibson
Paul Gibson
Frank Gilhooley
Charles Gipson
Joe Girardi
Fred Glade
Frank Gleich
Joe Glenn
Lefty Gómez
Jesse Gonder
Alberto Gonzalez
Fernando Gonzalez
Pedro Gonzalez
Wilbur Good
Dwight Gooden
Art Goodwin
Tom Gordon
Joe Gordon
Tom Gorman
Rich Gossage
Dick Gossett
Larry Gowell
Johnny Grabowski
Mike Grace
Alex Graman
Wayne Granger
Ted Gray
Eli Grba
Nick Green
Todd Greene
Paddy Greene

Ken Griffey, Sr.
Mike Griffin
Clark Griffith
Bob Grim
Burleigh Grimes
Oscar Grimes
Jason Grimsley
Lee Grissom
Buddy Groom
Cecilio Guante
Lee Guetterman
Ron Guidry
Aaron Guiel
Rudy Guillen
Brad Gulden
Don Gullett
Bill Gullickson
Randy Gumpert
Larry Gura

H

John Habyan
Bump Hadley
Kent Hadley
Noodles Hahn
Ed Hahn
Hinkey Haines
George Halas
Bob Hale
Jimmie Hall
Mel Hall
Brad Halsey
Roger Hambright
Steve Hamilton
Chris Hammond
Mike Handiboe
Jim Hanley
Truck Hannah
Ron Hansen
Harry Hanson
Jim Hardin
Bubbles Hargrave
Harry Harper
Toby Harrah
Greg A. Harris
Joe Harris
Jim Ray Hart
Roy Hartzell
Buddy Hassett
Ron Hassey
Andy Hawkins
Chicken Hawks
Charlie Hayes
Fran Healy
Mike Heath

Neal Heaton
Don Heffner
Mike Hegan
Fred Heimach
Woodie Held
Charlie Hemphill
Rollie Hemsley
Bill Henderson
Rickey Henderson
Harvey Hendrick
Ellie Hendricks
Tim Hendryx
Sean Henn
Tommy Henrich
Bill Henry
Drew Henson
Félix Heredia
Xavier Hernandez
Orlando Hernández
Adrian Hernandez
Michel Hernandez
Leo Hernández
Ed Herrmann
Hugh High
Oral Hildebrand
Jesse Hill
Glenallen Hill
Shawn Hillegas
Frank Hiller
Mack Hillis
Rich Hinton
Sterling Hitchcock
Myril Hoag
Butch Hobson
Chet Hoff
Danny Hoffman
Solly Hofman
Fred Hofmann
Bill Hogg
Bobby Hogue
Ken Holcombe
Bill Holden
Al Holland
Ken Holloway
Darren Holmes
Fred Holmes
Roger Holt
Ken Holtzman
Rick Honeycutt
Wally Hood
Don Hood
Johnny Hopp
Shags Horan
Ralph Houk
Elston Howard
Matt Howard

Steve Howe
Harry Howell
Jay Howell
Dick Howser
Waite Hoyt
Rex Hudler
Charles Hudson
Tom Hughes
Tom L. Hughes
Phil Hughes
Keith Hughes
John Hummel
Mike Humphreys
Ken Hunt
Catfish Hunter
Billy Hunter
Mark Hutton
Ham Hyatt

I

Kei Igawa
Pete Incaviglia
Hideki Irabu

J

Fred Jacklitsch
Austin Jackson
Grant Jackson
Reggie Jackson
Johnny James
Dion James
Stan Javier
Domingo Jean
Stan Jefferson
Jackie Jensen
Mike Jerzembeck
Derek Jeter
D'Angelo Jiménez
Elvio Jiménez
Brett Jodie
Tommy John
Alex Johnson
Billy Johnson
Cliff Johnson
Darrell Johnson
Deron Johnson
Don Johnson
Ernie Johnson
Hank Johnson
Jeff Johnson
Johnny Johnson
Ken Johnson
Lance Johnson
Nick Johnson

Otis Johnson
Randy Johnson
Russ Johnson
Roy Johnson
Jay Johnstone
Darryl Jones
Gary Jones
Jimmy Jones
Mitch Jones
Ruppert Jones
Sad Sam Jones
Tim Jordan
Art Jorgens
Félix José
Jeff Juden
Mike Jurewicz
David Justice

K

Jim Kaat
Scott Kamieniecki
Bob Kammeyer
Frank Kane
Bill Karlon
Herb Karpel
Steve Karsay
Jeff Karstens
Benny Kauff
Curt Kaufman
Eddie Kearse
Ray Keating
Bobby Keefe
Willie Keeler
Randy Keisler
Mike Kekich
Charlie Keller
Pat Kelly
Roberto Kelly
Steve Kemp
Ian Kennedy
John Kennedy
Jerry Kenney
Matt Keough
Jimmy Key
Steve Kiefer
Harry Kingman
Dave Kingman
Fred Kipp
Frank Kitson
Ron Kittle
Ted Kleinhans
Red Kleinow
Ed Klepfer
Ron Klimkowski
Steve Kline

Mickey Klutts
Bill Knickerbocker
Brandon Knight
John Knight
Chuck Knoblauch
Mark Koenig
Jim Konstanty
Andy Kosco
Steve Kraly
Jack Kramer
Ernie Krueger
Dick Kryhoski
Tony Kubek
Johnny Kucks
Bill Kunkel
Bob Kuzava

L

Dave LaRoche
Joe Lake
Bill Lamar
Hal Lanier
Eddi Lantigua
Dave LaPoint
Frank LaPorte
Don Larsen
Lyn Lary
Chris Latham
Marcus Lawton
Matt Lawton
Gene Layden
Tony Lazzeri
Jalal Leach
Tim Leary
Ricky Ledée
Travis Lee
Joe Lefebvre
Al Leiter
Mark Leiter
Frank Leja
Jack Lelivelt
Eddie Leon
Louis Leroy
Ed Levy
Duffy Lewis
Jim Lewis
Terry Ley
Jim Leyritz
Cory Lidle
Jon Lieber
Ted Lilly
Paul Lindblad
Johnny Lindell
Phil Linz
Bryan Little

Jack Little
Clem Llewellyn
Graeme Lloyd
Esteban Loaiza
Gene Locklear
Kenny Lofton
Tim Lollar
Sherm Lollar
Phil Lombardi
Dale Long
Herman Long
Terrence Long
Eddie Lopat
Art Lopez
Gabriel Lopez
Héctor López
Baldy Louden
Slim Love
Kevin Lovingier
Torey Lovullo
Mike Lowell
Johnny Lucadello
Joe Lucey
Roy Luebbe
Matt Luke
Jerry Lumpe
Scott Lusader
Sparky Lyle
Al Lyons
Jim Lyttle

M

Duke Maas
Kevin Maas
Rob MacDonald
Danny MacFayden
Ray Mack
Tommy Madden
Elliott Maddox
Hector Made
Dave Madison
Lee Magee
Sal Maglie
Stubby Magner
Jim Magnuson
Fritz Maisel
Hank Majeski
Frank Makosky
Pat Malone
Pat Maloney
Al Mamaux
Rube Manning
Mickey Mantle
Jeff Manto
Josias Manzanillo

Cliff Mapes
Roger Maris
Cliff Markle
Jim Marquis
Armando Marsans
Cuddles Marshall
Sam Marsonek
Billy Martin
Jack Martin
Hersh Martin
Tippy Martinez
Mike Martinez
Tino Martinez
Jim Mason
Victor Mata
Hideki Matsui
Don Mattingly
Rudy May
Darrell May
Carlos May
John Mayberry
Carl Mays
Lee Mazzilli
Larry McCall
Joe McCarthy
Pat McCauley
Larry McClure
George McConnell
Mike McCormick
Lance McCullers
Lindy McDaniel
Mickey McDermott
Danny McDevitt
Jim McDonald
Dave McDonald
Donzell McDonald
Gil McDougald
Sam McDowell
Jack McDowell
Lou McEvoy
Herm McFarland
Andy McGaffigan
Lynn McGlothen
Bob McGraw
Deacon McGuire
Marty McHale
Irish McIlveen
Tim McIntosh
Bill McKechnie
Rich McKinney
Frank McManus
Norm McMillan
Tommy McMillan
Mike McNally
Herb McQuaid
George McQuinn

Bobby Meacham
Charlie Meara
Jim Mecir
Doc Medich
Bob Melvin
Ramiro Mendoza
Fred Merkle
Andy Messersmith
Tom Metcalf
Bud Metheny
Hensley Meulens
Bob Meusel
Bob Meyer
Dan Miceli
Gene Michael
Ezra Midkiff
Doug Mientkiewicz
Pete Mikkelsen
Larry Milbourne
Sam Militello
Bill Miller
Elmer Miller
John Miller
Alan Mills
Buster Mills
Mike Milosevich
Paul Mirabella
Juan Miranda
Willy Miranda
Bobby Mitchell
Fred Mitchell
Johnny Mitchell
Johnny Mize
Kevin Mmahat
George Mogridge
Dale Mohorcic
Fenton Mole
Jose Molina
Bill Monbouquette
Raúl Mondesí
Ed Monroe
Zach Monroe
John Montefusco
Rich Monteleone
Archie Moore
Earl Moore
Wilcy Moore
Ray Morehart
Omar Moreno
Mike Morgan
Tom Morgan
George Moriarty
Jeff Moronko
Hal Morris
Ross Moschitto
Jerry Moses

Terry Mulholland
Charlie Mullen
Jerry Mumphrey
Bob Muncrief
Bobby Munoz
Thurman Munson
Bobby Murcer
Johnny Murphy
Rob Murphy
Dale Murray
George Murray
Larry Murray
Mike Mussina
Mike Myers

N

Jerry Narron
Dan Naulty
Dioner Navarro
Denny Neagle
Bots Nekola
Luke Nelson
Gene Nelson
Jeff Nelson
Graig Nettles
Tex Neuer
Ernie Nevel
Floyd Newkirk
Bobo Newsom
Doc Newton
Gus Niarhos
Carl Nichols
Phil Niekro
Joe Niekro
Scott Nielsen
Jerry Nielsen
Wil Nieves
Harry Niles
C. J. Nitkowski
Otis Nixon
Matt Nokes
Irv Noren
Don Nottebart
Les Nunamaker
Eduardo Nunez

O

Mike O'Berry
Andy O'Connor
Jack O'Connor
Paddy O'Connor
Lefty O'Doul
Steve O'Neill
Paul O'Neill

Queenie O'Rourke
Johnny Oates
Heinie Odom
Rowland Office
Bob Ojeda
Rube Oldring
John Olerud
Bob Oliver
Joe Oliver
Nate Oliver
Jesse Orosco
Al Orth
Donovan Osborne
Champ Osteen
Joe Ostrowski
Antonio Osuna
Bill Otis
Stubby Overmire
Spike Owen

P

John Pacella
Del Paddock
Juan Padilla
Dave Pagan
Joe Page
Mike Pagliarulo
Donn Pall
Clay Parker
Christian Parker
David Parrish
Ben Paschal
Dan Pasqua
Gil Patterson
Jeff Patterson
Mike Patterson
Carl Pavano
Dave Pavlas
Monte Pearson
Roger Peckinpaugh
Steve Peek
Hipolito Pena
Ramiro Pena
Herb Pennock
Joe Pepitone
Marty Perez
Melido Perez
Pascual Perez
Robert Perez
Cecil Perkins
Cy Perkins
Gaylord Perry
Fritz Peterson
Andy Pettitte
Ken Phelps

Josh Phelps
Andy Phillips
Eddie Phillips
Jack Phillips
Cy Pieh
Bill Piercy
Duane Pillette
Lou Piniella
George Pipgras
Wally Pipp
Jim Pisoni
Eric Plunk
Dale Polley
Luis Polonia
Sidney Ponson
Bob Porterfield
Jorge Posada
Scott Pose
Jack Powell
Jake Powell
Doc Powers
Del Pratt
Jerry Priddy
Curtis Pride
Johnny Priest
Chris Prieto
Bret Prinz
Scott Proctor
Alfonso Pulido
Ambrose Puttmann

Q

Paul Quantrill
Mel Queen
Eddie Quick
Jack Quinn
Jamie Quirk

R

Tim Raines
Dave Rajsich
Edwar Ramirez
Pedro Ramos
Bobby Ramos
John Ramos
Domingo Ramos
Len Randle
Willie Randolph
Vic Raschi
Dennis Rasmussen
Darrell Rasner
Shane Rawley
Jeff Reardon
Tim Redding

Jack Reed
Jimmie Reese
Kevin Reese
Hal Reniff
Bill Renna
Tony Rensa
Roger Repoz
Rick Reuschel
Dave Revering
Al Reyes
Allie Reynolds
Bill Reynolds
Rick Rhoden
Gordon Rhodes
Harry Rice
Bobby Richardson
Nolen Richardson
Branch Rickey
Dave Righetti
José Rijo
Danny Rios
Juan Rivera
Mariano Rivera
Rubén Rivera
Mickey Rivers
Phil Rizzuto
Roxey Roach
Dale Roberts
Gene Robertson
Andre Robertson
Aaron Robinson
Bill Robinson
Bruce Robinson
Eddie Robinson
Hank Robinson
Jeff Robinson
Alex Rodriguez
Aurelio Rodríguez
Carlos Rodriguez
Edwin Rodriguez
Ellie Rodríguez
Felix Rodriguez
Henry Rodriguez
Gary Roenicke
Oscar Roettger
Tom Rogers
Kenny Rogers
Jay Rogers
Jim Roland
Red Rolfe
Buddy Rosar
Larry Rosenthal
Steve Roser
Braggo Roth
Jerry Royster
Muddy Ruel

Dutch Ruether
Red Ruffing
Allan Russell
Marius Russo
Babe Ruth
Rosy Ryan
Blondy Ryan

S

Johnny Sain
Lenn Sakata
Mark Salas
Jack Saltzgaver
Bill Sample
Celerino Sanchez
Rey Sánchez
Roy Sanders
Deion Sanders
Scott Sanderson
Charlie Sands
Fred Sanford
Rafael Santana
Omir Santos
Bronson Sardinha
Don Savage
Rick Sawyer
Steve Sax
Ray Scarborough
Germany Schaefer
Harry Schaeffer
Roy Schalk
Art Schallock
Wally Schang
Bob Schmidt
Butch Schmidt
Johnny Schmitz
Pete Schneider
Dick "Ducky" Schofield
Paul Schreiber
Art Schult
Al Schulz
Don Schulze
Bill Schwarz
Pi Schwert
Everett Scott
George Scott
Rodney Scott
Rod Scurry
Scott Seabol
Ken Sears
Bob Seeds
Kal Segrist
Fernando Seguignol
George Selkirk
Ted Sepkowski

Hank Severeid
Joe Sewell
Howie Shanks
Bobby Shantz
Billy Shantz
Bob Shawkey
Spec Shea
Al Shealy
George Shears
Tom Sheehan
Gary Sheffield
Rollie Sheldon
Skeeter Shelton
Roy Sherid
Pat Sheridan
Dennis Sherrill
Ben Shields
Steve Shields
Bob Shirley
Urban Shocker
Tom Shopay
Ernie Shore
Bill Short
Norm Siebern
Rubén Sierra
Charlie Silvera
Ken Silvestri
Dave Silvestri
Hack Simmons
Harry Simpson
Dick Simpson
Duke Sims
Bill Skiff
Joel Skinner
Camp Skinner
Lou Skizas
Bill "Moose" Skowron
Roger Slagle
Don Slaught
Enos Slaughter
Aaron Small
Roy Smalley
Walt Smallwood
Charley Smith
Elmer Smith
Joe Smith
Keith Smith
Klondike Smith
Lee Smith
Matt Smith
Harry Smythe
J. T. Snow
Eric Soderholm
Luis Sojo
Tony Solaita
Alfonso Soriano

Steve Souchock
Jim Spencer
Shane Spencer
Charlie Spikes
Russ Springer
Bill Stafford
Jake Stahl
Roy Staiger
Tuck Stainback
Gerry Staley
Charley Stanceu
Andy Stankiewicz
Mike Stanley
Fred Stanley
Mike Stanton
Dick Starr
Dave Stegman
Dutch Sterrett
Bud Stewart
Lee Stine
Kelly Stinnett
Snuffy Stirnweiss
Tim Stoddard
Mel Stottlemyre
Hal Stowe
Darryl Strawberry
Gabby Street
Marlin Stuart
Bill Stumpf
Tom Sturdivant
Johnny Sturm
Tanyon Sturtze
Bill Sudakis
Steve Sundra
Dale Sveum
Ed Sweeney
Ron Swoboda

T

Fred Talbot
Vito Tamulis
Frank Tanana
Jesse Tannehill
Tony Tarasco
Danny Tartabull
Wade Taylor
Zack Taylor
Frank Tepedino
Walt Terrell
Ralph Terry
Jay Tessmer
Dick Tettelbach
Bob Tewksbury
Marcus Thames
Ira Thomas

Lee Thomas
Myles Thomas
Stan Thomas
Gary Thomasson
Homer Thompson
Kevin Thompson
Ryan Thompson
Tommy Thompson
Jack Thoney
Hank Thormahlen
Marv Throneberry
Mike Thurman
Luis Tiant
Dick Tidrow
Bobby Tiefenauer
Eddie Tiemeyer
Ray Tift
Bob Tillman
Thad Tillotson
Dan Tipple
Wayne Tolleson
Earl Torgeson
Rusty Torres
Mike Torrez
César Tovar
Bubba Trammell
Tom Tresh
Gus Triandos
Steve Trout
Virgil Trucks
Frank Truesdale
Bob Turley
Jim Turner
Chris Turner

U

George Uhle
Tom Underwood
Bob Unglaub
Cecil Upshaw

V

Marc Valdes
Elmer Valo
Russ Van Atta
Dazzy Vance
Joe Vance
John Vander Wal
Hippo Vaughn
Bobby Vaughn
Javier Vázquez
Bobby Veach
Marcos Vechionacci
Randy Velarde

Otto Vélez
Mike Vento
Robin Ventura
Jose Veras
Jose Veras
Joe Verbanic
Frank Verdi
Sammy Vick
Ron Villone
Ron Villone
José Vizcaíno
Luis Vizcaíno

W

Jake Wade
Dick Wakefield
Jim Walewander
Curt Walker
Dixie Walker
Mike Wallace
Dave Walling
Joe Walsh
Jimmy Walsh
Roxy Walters
Danny Walton
Paul Waner
Chien-Ming Wang
Jack Wanner
Pee-Wee Wanninger
Aaron Lee Ward
Gary Ward
Joe Ward
Pete Ward
Jack Warhop
George Washburn
Claudell Washington
Gary Waslewski
B.J. Waszgis
Allen Watson
Bob Watson
Roy Weatherly
David Weathers
Jim Weaver
Jeff Weaver
Dave Wehrmeister
Lefty Weinert
David Wells
Ed Wells
Butch Wensloff
Julie Wera
Billy Werber
Dennis Werth
Jake Westbrook
John Wetteland
Stefan Wever

Kevin Whelan
Steve Whitaker
Gabe White
Roy White
Rondell White
Wally Whitehurst
George Whiteman
Mark Whiten
Terry Whitfield
Ed Whitson
Kemp Wicker
Al Wickland
Bob Wickman
Chris Widger
Bob Wiesler
Bill Wight
Ted Wilborn
Ed Wilkinson
Bernie Williams
Bob Williams
Gerald Williams
Harry Williams
Jimmy Williams
Stan Williams
Todd Williams
Walt Williams
Archie Wilson
Craig Wilson
Enrique Wilson
George Wilson
Kris Wilson
Pete Wilson
Snake Wiltse
Gordie Windhorn
Dave Winfield
Jay Witasick
Mickey Witek
Mike Witt

Whitey Witt
Mark Wohlers
Barney Wolfe
Harry Wolter
Harry Wolverton
Dooley Womack
Tony Womack
Gene Woodling
Ron Woods
Dick Woodson
Eric Wordekemper
Hank Workman
Ken Wright
Jaret Wright
Chase Wright
Yats Wuestling
John Wyatt
Butch Wynegar
Jimmy Wynn

Y

Ed Yarnall
Joe Yeager
Jim York
Curt Young
Ralph Young

Z

Tom Zachary
Jack Zalusky
George Zeber
Rollie Zeider
Todd Zeile
Guy Zinn
Bill Zuber
Paul Zuvella